THE COMPLETE
SKIER

THE COMPLETE
SKIER

A practical guide for skiers of all levels

KAREN & MICHAEL LIEBREICH

BBC BOOKS

Karen and Michael Liebreich learnt to ski in Czechoslovakia as young children. Michael has been in the British Freestyle Ski Team since 1987, and was British moguls champion in 1988. Since then he has been among the country's top three moguls skiers. He has represented Britain at World Cup events since 1988 and at the Winter Olympics in 1992. Michael combines his competitive skiing with a career as a management consultant, having earned an MBA at Harvard.
Karen has also skied extensively, and is a keen ski tourer. Away from the slopes she is a writer and broadcaster with a doctorate in history.

Published by BBC Books,
a division of BBC Enterprises Limited,
Woodlands, 80 Wood Lane
London W12 OTT

First published 1993
© Karen and Michael Liebreich 1993
ISBN 0 563 36380 0

Designed by Bob Gordon
Set in Caslon Open Face and Joanna
Printed and bound in Great Britain by BPCC Paulton Books Ltd
Colour separation by Technik Ltd, Berkhamsted
Cover printed by Richard Clays Ltd, St Ives PLC

ACKNOWLEDGEMENTS

During the writing of this book, one of the authors was constantly on the road, taking part in international ski competitions; the other was pregnant. That this book was ever completed is due in no small part to the help we received. Our thanks go to Heather Holden-Brown for believing that we could do it, to Nicky Copeland for managing the busiest and most geographically dispersed co-authors ever, to Bob Gordon for patiently dealing with endless revisions and to the rest of the team at BBC Books.

In writing the technical chapters, we received much valuable help from Stevie Newlands, British Association of Ski Instructors (BASI) trainer, and Gil Palter, member of the Canadian Ski Instructors' Alliance (CSIA). Any remaining mistakes or confusions are purely our own. The fitness and warm-up sections owe much to the advice of Karen Flury, MCSP, SRP (physiotherapist to the British Freestyle Ski Team) and fitness consultant Jan Bennett, PEA, RSA. Edward J. Spearing, of the British Snowboarding Association helped us with snowboarding, and Dane Weis

(Ski 47) with equipment. The Ski Club of Great Britain provided us with information and library access, and Bob Kinnaird, Chief Executive of BASI, with constructive advice. David Levin was a thorough and spirited proofreader.

During the research and photo-shoot for this book, hospitality and scenery were provided by the following resorts: Les Arcs, Avoriaz, Chamonix, Courmayeur, Megève, Meribel, Val d'Isère and Verbier. Many thanks to Mark Warner for the use of their crèche facilities. We would also like to thank all those who helped out with clothing or equipment: Salomon GB (ski boots and bindings); Ultrasport/Rossignol (skis); Leki (poles); Degré 7, Berghaus and Phoenix/Gore-Tex (clothing); Bollé (sunglasses and goggles); Hestra (gloves); Lowe (fleeces); Sport Extrême of Chamonix (demonstration equipment); Vulkan (knee braces); and Fagans (Bauer In-Line Skates).

Michael would like to take this opportunity to thank all those who have played an important role in his skiing career: Major R. J. Smith of the

US Air Force, who first took him into the bumps; Sarah Morrison, who gave him his first chance in international competition; Rob Morrison, the long-suffering coach of the British Freestyle Ski Team; everyone at the British Ski Federation; and everyone at McKinsey & Company, who made it possible for him to go to the Albertville Olympics. Karen would like to thank David Dawson-Pick for his support and understanding as she worked on this manuscript.

This book would never have appeared had it not been for Jeremy, who not only contributed the chapter on the medical aspects of skiing, but also took on the unenviable and dangerous role of arbitrator between us. Many were the arguments interrupted by his expertly-timed catering. Our thanks too to Laura, for her proofreading and patience. Finally, these acknowledgements would not be complete without thanking our grandparents and parents, who took us skiing so often over the years and imparted to us a love of their favourite sport, and to baby Sam for remaining asleep while we discussed these acknowledgements.

CONTENTS

Karen and Michael Liebreich

INTRODUCTION

Skiing is a great sport. It offers a unique combination of exhilaration, challenge and access to the mountains. It is clearly one of the best things in life.

Good skiers paint relaxed, precise turns on the canvas of the mountain. Their skiing is powerful and balanced. They can cope with any slope, in any conditions. Their legs work independently under a calm upper body, and they perform no superfluous movements. They are safe, respecting the mountains around them, and are aware of their own limitations.

Learning to ski should not be a frustrating experience. Yet too often, it seems that fashions in technique come and go, and what is described as a 'must learn' one season is consigned to the scrap-heap the next.

At whatever level you find yourself, this book tries to point out the next steps down the path, letting you know which skills you need to develop, and describing techniques and exercises that will lead to those skills. In this way, it hopes to dispel a little anxiety and ease your transition into the world of better skiing.

We hope you find this book helpful. But never forget that skiing is about more than technique; it is also about finding ways of enjoying the challenge and beauty of the mountains without destroying them.

KAREN & MICHAEL LIEBREICH

1 · THE HISTORY OF SKIING

The first evidence of skiing comes from Scandinavia, where it was used
as a method of transport during the long, snowbound months of winter
over 4000 years ago. Its spread was primarily due to its military
value until the last two centuries, but now it has blossomed into a
popular sport and a multi-billion pound industry.

FROM THE FIRST SKIER TO TODAY

PREHISTORY

Skis were first used in prehistoric times to enable man to continue his hunter-gatherer existence throughout winter.

c.2500BC

Oldest known ski lost in a Scandinavian peat-bog. The Hoting ski resurfaced millennia later.

c.2000BC

Earliest known picture of skiers. A cave wall in Tjoetta, Norway, provided the backdrop for an artist's drawing of colleagues using skis to hunt elk.

EARLY HISTORY

During this period, many legends and myths grew up around those who were skilled on skis.

AD550

'Gliding Finns' won fame after using unorthodox methods of transport in battle. Described by Procopius in *De Bello Gothico*.

c.880

King Harald Harfagr praises Vighard for the first recorded schuss.

c.1200

Saga of Kalevala: the hero of this Finnish epic skied so fast that his ski pole apparently smoked in the snow.

c.1222

First marriage break-up caused by skiing described by Icelandic bard Snorre Sturlason. The goddess Skadi abandoned her husband, the god Njord, to go skiing.

Early Norwegian skier, 2000 BC.

SIXTEENTH TO EIGHTEENTH CENTURIES

During the sixteenth, seventeenth and eighteenth centuries, the use of skis spread rapidly as they proved their military usefulness.

1520

First ski marathon. The Swedes refused to follow Gustav Vasa and rebel against the ruling Danes. When he abandoned them in disgust, they sent their best skiers after him to beg him to return. Their effort is commemorated each year in the 85km (53mile) Vasaloppet race.

1549

The existence of skiing outside Scandinavia is acknowledged by Sigmund Freiherr von Herberstein in *Rerum Moscoviticarum commentarii.*

1602

Norwegian ski troops used in fighting against the Russians.

1713

First recorded use of baskets on ski poles.

1774

Competition with prize money held for Norwegian military skiers.

NINETEENTH CENTURY

By the nineteenth century, skiing was being practised for enjoyment, and no longer merely for functional reasons.

1840s-50s

Skiing introduced into Australia and the United States by Norwegian and Swedish gold miners.

With one long 'glider' and one short 'pusher', this seventeenth-century skier used a skating technique and only one pole to go hunting.

1860

Invention of the tuck position in La Porte, United States. Tommy Todd set the first speed skiing record of 130kph (80mph) on 4m skis.

1866

Christiania turn and parallel stop perfected by Sondre Norheim, from Telemark in Norway. He improved his skis' manoeuvrability by cutting them down to 2m40 and carving a waist into them. He also made improvements to his bindings, though he retained the use of a single pole. Norheim is also credited with inventing the telemark turn.

1883

Skis used by monks at the St Bernard Pass. Their most famous dog, Barry, later gave his name to the Barryvox, a make of avalanche safety transceiver.

1888

Greenland traversed on skis by Norwegian Fridtjof Nansen. His account fired the imagination of skiers across Europe.

1891

First ski club founded, in Germany.

1896

Snowplough turn invented by Austrian Matthias Zdarsky, who has been called 'the father of alpine skiing'. He shortened his 3m Norwegian skis to 1m80, got rid of the groove and the nipples at the tips, and fixed his heel to the ski. As a result he could negotiate the steep terrain of the Alps, and his Lilienfelder Schilauf-Technik formed the basis of Austrian theory for many years.

Nansen's adventure helped to popularize skiing.

TWENTIETH CENTURY, PREWAR

The period before the Second World War was characterized by a rapid rise in the popularity of the sport, and a corresponding improvement in equipment. Ski competition developed as a means of settling debates about the pros and cons of alternative techniques.

1903
First competition in the Alps (Public Schools Alpine Sports Club Challenge) organized by Arnold Lunn, pillar of the British skiing establishment. Use of sticks for braking was not allowed. Ski Club of Great Britain founded.

1909
Stem Christiania turn developed by Hannes Schneider from Arlberg, Austria, allowing him to achieve previously impossible speeds.

1910
Use of the snowplough and two poles promoted by Colonel Bilgeri of the Imperial Austrian army.

1921
First British Championships organized by Arnold Lunn. Competition consisted of both downhill and style disciplines, although the latter was soon discarded due to judging difficulty.

1924
First Winter Olympics held in Chamonix. Athletes competed in 'nordic' disciplines – cross-country and jumping. The Fédération Internationale de Ski (FIS) was founded to regulate the sport.

1927
First association of professional ski teachers established in Austria.

1930
First use of steel ski edges by Rudolph Lettner of Salzburg. His grip on the snow was immeasurably enhanced.

1932
First drag lift built by Gerhard Mueller of Switzerland, using a rope and a motorbike engine. In the States, Jim Curran invented the chair lift.

1936
Slalom and downhill racing included for the first time in the Olympics at Garmisch Partenkirchen.

1937
Emile Allais won the FIS downhill and slalom using parallel technique. A great debate followed, which was to last for over 40 years: the Austrian school vs the French school, the stem turn vs the parallel turn, the knees vs the hips.

1938
British attention turned to French resorts, leaving Austria to Hitler. Colonel Peter Lindsay encouraged investment in the Trois Vallées.

1939
Hannes Schneider took refuge from Nazism in the US, taking with him the Austrian technique. The expression 'Bend ze knees' became a cliché of ski instruction.

The Swedish Crown Princess (third from right) and court take to the slopes.

TWENTIETH CENTURY, POSTWAR

As prosperity returned after the dislocation of the Second World War, people once again took to the slopes. This was the period of rapid development of resorts and lift systems for the mass skiing market.

1946

First teleski in the Trois Vallées, France and opening of Lift One in Aspen, Colorado.

1948

First experiments with artificial snow-making carried out in Connecticut.

1950

First commercial production of metal skis. After years of experimentation, Howard Head, an aerospace engineer, finally succeeded in producing a wood/plastic/aluminium laminated ski that did not fall apart instantly. The black Head Standards were soon dubbed 'cheaters' because they turned so easily.

1950s

Stretch pants invented by the German Bogner family. Skiing was confirmed as a glamour sport. First safety bindings produced by Hannes Marker.

1952

Giant slalom added to the Oslo Olympic programme.

Mid-1950s

Austrian skiers, including Toni Sailer, dominated the racing scene. Wedeln, defined by skiing guru Professor Kruckenhauser as 'parallel turning in quick succession using reverse shoulder and heel pressure,' became all the rage.

1955

Clips began to replace laces as fastenings on ski boots.

Late 1950s

Frenchmen Georges Joubert and Jean Vuarnet broke the Austrians' hold with their new turn, the Christiania léger.

1967

First plastic boot produced by Bob Lange. The days of damp leather boots were over.

1968

Jean-Claude Killy won gold medals in all three alpine disciplines at the Grenoble Olympics.

1970s

Explosion of popularity of the sport due to easier-turning skis, moulded boots and package holidays. First use of fibreglass in ski construction by Austrian Franz Kneissl. Ingemar Stenmark became the most successful alpine skier ever with 86 World Cup victories.

The 1980s and 1990s

During the 1980s, skiing matured into a major sport and leisure industry throughout Europe, the United States and Japan. New materials, such as carbon fibre, titanium and Kevlar continued to improve ski equipment, while new fabrics and insulating materials improved ski clothing, offering skiers increased comfort and freedom.

Novel ways of sliding appeared, offering a challenge for those jaded by normal skiing. Monoskis, mini-skis, ski-scooters and hang-gliders all enjoyed a boom; parapenting and snowboarding became established as major sports, and telemarking enjoyed a rebirth.

In competition, freestyle skiing grew in popularity, with ballet, moguls and aerials demonstrated at the 1988 Calgary Olympics. Moguls achieved full medal status at the 1992 Albertville Olympics, France; aerials in 1994 at Lillehammer, Norway.

Meanwhile, the environmental cost of the sport began to make itself felt. With some 40000 runs and 14000 lifts in the European Alps, and with tourists spending around 250 million holiday days there annually, the region began to show increasing signs of pressure. In Europe and the United States, environmental considerations all but put a stop to the expansion of ski areas.

Skiers are now increasingly reminding themselves that skiing is not only about speed and physical exertion, but also about appreciating nature and the surrounding mountainscape. Touring, heli-skiing, skiing in exotic locations and other ways of getting away from the herd are all growing in popularity.

Gary Cooper and Clark Gable contributed to skiing's jet set image.

2 · GETTING FIT TO SKI

Skiing is a demanding sport. It subjects your body to repeated stresses and involves strenuous exertion at high altitudes. The fitter you are, the better and longer you will be able to ski each day, the lower your risk of injury will be, and the more you will enjoy your holiday.

A ski fitness programme should be designed to achieve several aims. Perhaps most importantly, skiing requires aerobic fitness, needed for exercise in the thin mountain air. It also, however, calls for anaerobic fitness, the strength and ability to sustain short bursts of exertion. Finally, your ski fitness programme should improve your co-ordination, balance and flexibility, allowing you a more dynamic range of movement.

You should concentrate on those muscle groups that are most used in skiing: the leg muscles, especially the quadriceps and hamstrings; the abdominals, which control body posture; and the triceps, which are used for poling.

Ski Fitness Programme

PREPARING FOR THE SLOPES

Use the exercises described here to prepare for your coming ski holiday. Each session consists of three elements:
1 warm-up
2 exercise circuits
3 stretch

Each session should take under an hour. Aim to train at least twice a week during the two months prior to your ski holiday, building the frequency during the last month.

If you have an existing injury about which you are worried, it is always better to protect it than to re-injure it. If in doubt about an old injury or a medical condition, consult your doctor or physiotherapist (see chapter 19, page 213).

1 WARM-UP (15 MINUTES)

Never start training without a warm-up. Jog gently on the spot for five minutes to get your circulation going. This will increase the blood flow to your muscles, warming and relaxing them. (Alternatively, use the pre-ski warm-up described on page 61.)

Then stretch the major muscle groups on both sides to prepare them for more vigorous use. The following exercises are static stretches, so there should be no bouncing, no getting out of breath, no straining. Hold each position for 10 seconds, and make sure you feel the stretch in the correct muscles. Pay particular attention to your back and knees, since these are vulnerable to injury.

Calves (gastrocnemius)
Lean against a wall and push. Keep your feet pointing forwards, with your heels on the floor, and back leg straight.

Calves (soleus)
Repeat the above exercise with your back knee bent.

Front of thighs (quadriceps)
Stand on one leg with the supporting leg slightly bent. Keep your knees together, hold onto a wall for support, and pull the other foot up to your buttocks.

Adductors (inside of thighs)
Stand with your legs apart, and push your hips to the left and right.

Hamstring
Stand with one foot advanced, and the back leg slightly bent. Keep your feet flat on the floor. Bring your weight forwards and rest your hands on your front knee for support.

Deltoids
Pull your arm across your body with the other hand on your elbow.

Triceps
Drop one arm behind your head, hold above the elbow with the other hand and pull.

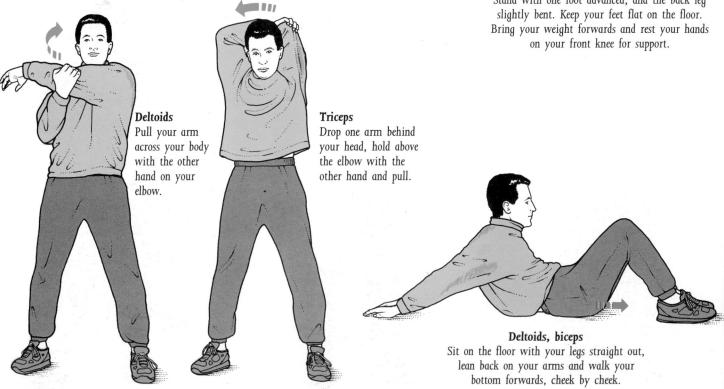

Deltoids, biceps
Sit on the floor with your legs straight out, lean back on your arms and walk your bottom forwards, cheek by cheek.

Shoulders
Clasp your hands behind you, push out and upwards.

Back
Sit on the floor, lock your hands under your knees and pull upwards.
Try to curl your back.

Neck
Rotate forwards and to both sides (but not backwards).

Wrists and hands
Flex your hand and fingers with the other hand.

2 EXERCISE CIRCUITS (20 MINUTES)

Each circuit consists of 12 exercises, taking around half a minute each. For each exercise, do the number of repetitions shown, then rest for half a minute. Concentrate on the quality of your execution, lowering the number of repetitions if you find any exercise particularly hard.

Start with one circuit, building to two or three as your holiday approaches. If you can find a partner with whom to train, it is more fun and easier to count and time your rest periods.

Be careful not to overdo it, particularly when you first start training.

Knee-bends (20)
Flex down through 45 degrees, then push back to standing. Keep your heels on the floor.

Jumps on the spot (20)

Abdominal raises (20)

Lie on your back on the floor, with slightly
bent legs, and hands clasped behind your head.
Lift your shoulders, keeping your lower back on
the floor. If you find this hard, cross your arms
on your chest or let them rest on your thighs.

Jumps to left and right (40)

Try to cover a reasonable distance
with each jump.

Leg raises (20)

Kneeling on all fours, bring one
knee in toward your chest, then
push the leg back behind you, toe
pointed. Raise the extended leg.
After 20, repeat with the other leg.

Triceps raises (20)

Sit on the floor with your knees bent and your palms on the floor behind your hips, fingers facing forward. Relax your stomach muscles and lower your body towards the floor, keeping your back straight. Bring your body up again by straightening your arms.

Abductor raises (20)

Lie on your side with both legs bent.
Raise the upper leg.
After 20, repeat with the other leg.

Dorsals (20)
Lie on your stomach with your arms in front of you. Lift your right arm and left leg off the ground simultaneously. After 20, repeat on the other side.

Lunges (20)
Lunge forwards onto one leg, flexing the knee through 45 degrees. Make sure your foot stays in line with your knee. Push back upright and lunge forwards onto the other leg.

Press-ups (20)
If you find these hard, do bent knee press-ups instead.

3 STRETCH (10 MINUTES)

Finish each training session with a thorough stretch, using exercises from the warm-up section (pages 21-23).

This helps to dissipate lactic acid and hence to avoid muscle pain. It is also essential for maintaining flexibility, which can be lost as part of the normal ageing process or as muscles develop. Repeat

stretches from the warm-up section but this time hold them for 30 seconds. Stretching should be done while the muscles are still warm, either from exercise or after a bath.

Year-round Fitness

LOOKING AFTER YOUR BODY

In order to get the most out of your skiing, keep your body in good shape throughout the year. Cycling, running, swimming and skipping are good for cardiovascular fitness, as are aerobic or stepping workouts. To improve your endurance, your fitness training should include at least 20 uninterrupted minutes of aerobic work, at least twice a week.

Squash and racquetball help to build explosive power, while weights are most effective to develop muscular strength. There is no need to use heavy weights, or to build muscle bulk. Concentrate on leg and back exercises, but don't forget your stomach and shoulders. Aim for three to six sets of 20 repetitions with fairly light weights, concentrating on perfect execution.

You can also improve your balance and co-ordination during the off season. Almost all active sports will help. If you want to work on your technique before your next trip to the snow, try grass skiing or visit your local dry slope. Roller-blading is fun and uses much of the same technique as carving turns on skis.

Roller-blading offers a fun way to stay fit and improve your balance. You can even work on your ski technique.

DRY SLOPES

GETTING A HEAD START

A very useful way to get ready for your approaching holiday is to visit your local dry ski slope.

Most older slopes are made of Dendix, which allows the skis to slide over a surface of toothbrush-like bristles. The sensation is not too dissimilar to skiing on spring snow, though gradient and terrain are limited. Newer slopes offer sophisticated attractions such as artificial snow. Some even offer moguls. No specialized skills are needed, and most techniques that you will use on piste can be practised on the dry slope.

Don't use your own skis, because you risk damaging them. If you have your own boots, this is a good time to ease your feet back into them. Wear old clothes, not your brand-new one-piece, and never ski without gloves.

If you have skied before, a dry slope offers you an opportunity to shake off the larger flakes of rust and to meet other keen skiers. If you are a complete beginner, you will have to take lessons.

A couple of sessions on a dry slope can give you a head start when it comes to your first days on snow. But remember 'real' skiing is much more fun, and a fall hurts less on snow, so don't let yourself be put off. At the very least you can learn how to put your skis on and what it feels like to slide on them. And it should be a fun day out.

A typical artificial slope.

3 · Choosing a Holiday

At first sight, the choice of different skiing holidays can seem overwhelming. The right decision depends on the type of skiing you are looking for, the type of resort and the size of your budget as well as a host of other variables, such as snow and travel conditions. There are, however, many sources of information to make your decision easier.

Your travel agent should be a good starting point. Alternatively, contact the tourist board of the chosen country. Each ski resort also has a tourist office, which can supply you with brochures, piste maps, lists of hotels and plans of the village. For package holidays and special offers, check the national press and skiing magazines. Above all, talk to other skiers to form an idea of the type of skiing holiday you would most enjoy.

WHICH COUNTRY TO CHOOSE?

Each country offers a slightly different holiday experience (see chapter 20, page 218 for a guide to resorts). The following list provides a stereotypical but handy rule of thumb.

Australia offers good, cheap accommodation and few queues, though alpine skiing is limited. But it might be an option for those who can't last through July to September without a skiing fix.

Austria provides traditional holidays in jolly, charming villages. Most of the visitors tend to be German.

Eastern Europe (the Czech and Slovak Republics, Bulgaria, Romania and Slovenia) provides limited but very cheap facilities. Standards of accommodation, instruction, rental and lift equipment may leave something to be desired.

France provides challenging skiing, with many resorts linking several valleys in huge ski areas. Avoid the school holidays when the whole country floods to the slopes.

Georgia and Russia share the Caucasus Mountains, the highest in Europe. Skiing can be fabulous, though the lift systems are under-developed and medical facilities, hotels, transport and communications can be dreadful.

Italy is relaxed and stylish, with good skiing and food. Resorts near to big cities are prone to overcrowding.

Japan offers good, though expensive skiing. Areas are frequently extremely crowded, signs are in Japanese and there may be few rental boots for Western bigfoots.

New Zealand is better for heli-skiing and cross-country than for alpine skiing. The season lasts from July to September.

Scandinavia has numerous small resorts that offer alpine skiing. It is expensive, but great for cross-country skiing and saunas.

Scotland enjoys miserable weather, but has some challenging skiing and a great nightlife.

South America offers good skiing during the Northern Hemisphere's summer months, for those prepared for long journeys.

Spain is appropriate for beginners and intermediates, with small, fairly cheap resorts.

Switzerland has the most stunning scenery, with well-organized, clean but expensive facilities.

United States and Canada offer large apartments, good facilities, orderly queues and friendly service. The east coast can be crowded, with hard, icy pistes. The Rocky Mountains (Colorado, Wyoming, Utah, New Mexico) are the place to go for really good powder.

WHAT IF THERE IS NO SNOW?

Snow cover depends on the season, the altitude and luck. The best plan is to choose your resort and time of year carefully – and then keep your fingers crossed. If you can ski only once a year, the safest and best time is late February to early March. Choose a high resort with glacier skiing, just in case. If you can afford to wait until nearer your departure date, many newspapers provide snow reports, and there are numerous snow hot-lines to ring for information. Remember, however, that it is not in the interests of the skiing industry to tell you that there isn't a flake in sight, so information may be somewhat over-optimistic. In addition, the reports are usually a couple of days out of date.

Many tour operators offer snow guarantees, although bear in mind that if you have to be bussed to the snow every day you will lose a lot of skiing time. Likewise, lift operators offer money-back guarantees if all the lifts are closed, but they are generally able to keep something open in all conditions to avoid that necessity.

Artificial snow is used increasingly to ensure that skiing can be offered throughout the season. However, the result is no substitute for adequate quantities of natural snow, so you shouldn't choose your holiday destination solely on the number of cannons used by the ski area.

Season and Altitude

WHEN TO GO

The following recommendations apply only to resorts in the Northern Hemisphere.

Pre-Christmas

There may not be much snow, except at the highest resorts or those equipped with snow cannons. However, if there have been a few snowstorms, good skiing can be found. Prices are low, but all facilities may not yet be open. Resort staff and shop assistants may treat customers like guinea pigs for the 'real' season.

Christmas and New Year

This is the peak skiing season and hence expensive. Snow is not guaranteed in any but the highest resorts, which tend to fill up immediately after Christmas.

January

Low season, with quiet resorts and fairly empty runs. This is generally the coldest month, but for keen skiers a good bet.

February

The ideal month in lower resorts, with sun and good snow conditions reflected in crowds and peak prices.

March

For higher resorts, this is the perfect month to ski, with long days, sun and good snow.

Easter

Good skiing conditions can be marred by high prices and crowds, especially around the local school holidays.

April onwards

Late spring can see some wonderful skiing, but choose a very high resort. This is the end of the season, and resort staff may be bored and unhelpful.

Summer skiing

A few days' skiing can offer an enjoyable break during the summer. Glacier skiing is generally available only in the mornings, before the snow becomes slushy and the lifts close. The afternoons are spent walking, playing tennis, wind-surfing or mountain-biking. Summer ski resorts include Hintertux and Kaprun in Austria, Tignes in France, Saas Fee and Zermatt in Switzerland, Mount Hood in the United States and Whistler in Canada.

SPEND, SPEND, SPEND

Unfortunately skiing is not a cheap sport. Accommodation, travel, ski pass, insurance, food and rental of equipment all add up, even without après-ski drinks thrown in. In general, the larger and more extensive the resort, the more expensive it will be. To keep your costs down:
- Avoid peak season.
- Scan the newspapers for last-minute special offers.
- Stay in a self-catered apartment.
- Stay a little further from the slopes or outside the village centre.
- Don't eat lunch at mountain restaurants.

HOW HIGH TO SKI

The altitude of a ski area is probably the most important single factor in determining the snow conditions you will find.

European skiing ranges from a few hundred metres above sea level in Norway (e.g. 180m (590ft) at Lillehammer) to over 3800m (12450 ft) at Chamonix's Aiguille du Midi. In North America, some of the highest skiing can be found at nearly 4000m (13000ft) at Colorado's Arapahoe is even higher.

The altitude of the resort itself is important, as is that of the highest lift. If you visit a resort in March that is situated just 1000m (3300ft) above sea level don't expect to be able to ski back home at the end of the day. If the summit of the lift system is below 1600m (5250ft), there may be no skiing at all in a poor season.

For a full picture of the type of skiing offered by a resort, you might check whether slopes face north or south, but this is time-consuming. Find out instead about the past snow record.

TYPE OF SKIING

BEGINNER

Choose a resort that is recommended for beginners. Has the ski school got a good reputation? Can the teachers speak English? Are the nursery slopes in the sun? Are they close to the resort? Don't go to a resort with scores of advanced runs, as you'll be paying for facilities you can't use.

INTERMEDIATE

Is there a good range of suitable runs? Does the resort cover a large ski area? How many lifts are there? Do they link to adjacent valleys?

ADVANCED

Is there a sufficient range of skiing to keep you happy for the whole holiday? Does the ski pass let you try other nearby resorts? Is there any good off-piste skiing? Does the resort tend to over-groom the slopes?

Piste maps are a good starting point when you are choosing a ski area. Extensive purpose-built French resorts, such as those in the Three Valleys (below), offer more variety than a smaller Andorran resort like Port Ainé (right), but at a price.

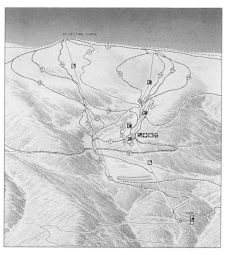

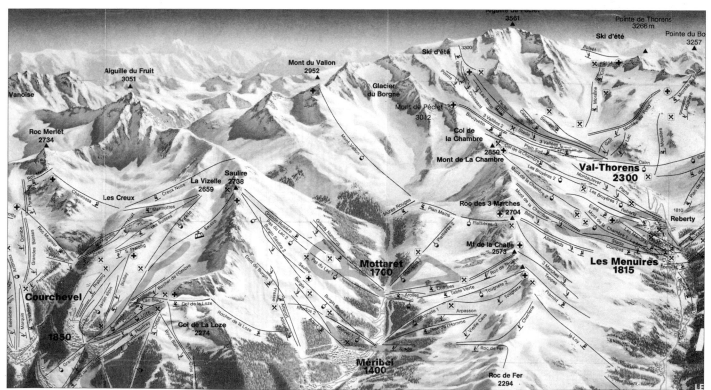

RESORT AND ACCOMMODATION

TYPE OF RESORT

In Europe, the debate tends to resolve itself into charm versus functionalism, although in recent years the borders have started to blur. As the older resorts rationalize their lift systems, and some of the newer resorts revert to wood-clad traditional architecture, differences may not be so significant in future.

The earliest ski villages were places like Zermatt and Chamonix, renowned for mountaineering before skiing became fashionable. Built at or below the tree-line - around 1800-2000m (5900-6560ft) in Europe - many of these resorts still cater for a large non-skiing clientele, with jewellery shops, fur coats and matching prices.

During the sixties and seventies resorts such as Avoriaz, Tignes or Les Menuires were purpose-built to cater for mass-market skiing. Their high-rise architecture does not appeal to everyone, but they are well located for excellent skiing, and you can usually ski to your door.

In North America, the diversity of villages is much more limited. Some resorts, such as Aspen or Jackson Hole, have a certain character, but none can approach the best of European chic. Instead they offer convenience, with good facilities, cheap food and a healthy, unpretentious nightlife. Note that to enjoy many ski areas, a car is indispensable.

Another consideration when choosing a resort is the location. How far is the resort from the airport? Is it worth flying across the Atlantic for just a week, when you may spend the first day travelling and the next two being jet-lagged? If going by car, can you park in the resort? Increasing numbers of resorts, such as Wengen and Zermatt, are car-free.

Purpose-built (below) vs traditional (right).

WHERE SHOULD YOU STAY?

There are several options on the accommodation front. The most luxurious is to stay in an hotel. Older European resorts, such as Zermatt and St Moritz, have splendid traditional hotels where you can easily spend a year's salary on a week's holiday. Most resorts have a selection of more reasonably priced hotels, offering half-board on a weekly basis.

Probably the cheapest option is to rent an apartment. In Europe, the purpose-built French resorts are best geared up for this, though the accommodation can be absurdly cramped. North American apartments tend to be much more comfortable. Rental periods generally run from Saturday to Saturday and you arrange your own transport. As food is expensive in ski resorts, stock up with supplies before reaching your destination.

A popular choice for British skiers is the chalet holiday. For a reasonable price, this offers flight, transfer from airport to resort, accommodation and food. Almost all contact with local cuisine or natives is, for better or for worse, eliminated. Accommodation may be rudimentary and, unless you can fill the whole chalet with friends, you may have to dine with bores, but it's a fairly hassle-free, cheap and cheerful way of organizing your skiing holiday.

Whichever option you choose, make sure your hotel, chalet or apartment is well located. How far is it from the centre of the village? How close to the nearest lift? How far from the bus stop?

4 · EQUIPMENT

Your equipment plays an important role in how you ski. As a beginner, your needs will change quickly; renting equipment at first saves money. As you improve, buying your own equipment makes increasing sense. Better shops rent material 'on test', subtracting the rental cost from the price of any eventual purchase. Read a few magazines beforehand so you can ask the right questions.

The secret of success in ski shops is to pick your moment: don't go during rush hour, because a busy sales assistant cannot give you the attention you need. If rental equipment offered is not in good condition, have it changed or go elsewhere – very few resorts have only one shop. And don't rent equipment at home for a holiday on the other side of the continent: if you have any problems, you'll be stuck.

As for clothes, again try to minimize your expenditure on your first trip. Some items can be borrowed: others, such as a good jacket, can be used for different sports and are worth buying. Some shops rent clothes as well as equipment.

Boots

What should you look for in a ski boot? Firstly, it must be comfortable: you will be wearing it for around seven hours a day, day in and day out. Secondly, the boot must form an effective link between you and the snow. It must be sufficiently rigid laterally to transmit movements of your legs into ski movements, but must still allow some forward flex at the ankle. Finally, it must hold your foot, and especially your heel, firmly in place.

The basic construction of all ski boots is similar, consisting of a rigid polyurethane shell, with a soft removable inner. Boots can be front-, rear- or mid-entry. Rear-entry boots are regarded as offering superior comfort and ease of fastening, and are an appropriate choice for a beginner. Front-entry provide optimum precision and control, while mid-entry boots profess to offer the advantages of both systems. Actual experience varies from boot to boot and from foot to foot, so make sure you try on a variety of boots.

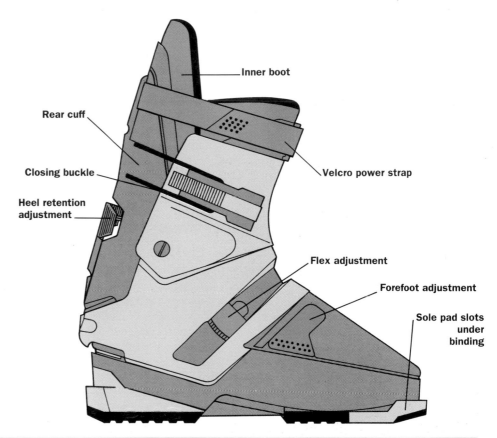

Inner boot

Rear cuff

Closing buckle

Heel retention adjustment

Velcro power strap

Flex adjustment

Forefoot adjustment

Sole pad slots under binding

FRONT- VS REAR- VS MID-ENTRY BOOTS

Rear- and mid-entry boots allow you to stand with a straight(ish) leg when not skiing. Front-entry boots purport to offer greater precision during skiing.

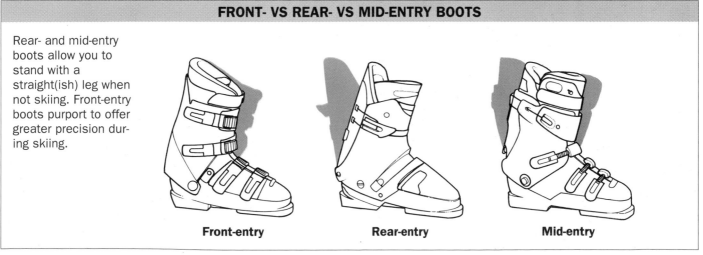

Front-entry

Rear-entry

Mid-entry

CHOICE OF MODEL

Select a model appropriate to your level, or at most the level you hope to be in two years. If you are an intermediate, there is little point wasting time and money on a racing model. Why use a Formula One to do the weekly shopping? For beginners a light, comfortable boot is best. It should have a fairly soft shin and flex, and should not be too sharply raked forwards. For experts a stiffer boot is required, with sufficient adjustments to optimize fit and control. If you are a decent skier, don't let the salesperson scare you into a comfortable, low-performance boot.

FIT

Since ski boots have such different requirements from other footwear, normal shoe sizes are not always used. Some manufacturers quote sizes by volume, some by the Mondo point system, which measures foot length in centimetres. The shop will measure you for whichever model you want to try. A half size smaller than your normal shoe size is usually recommended. Listen to the salesperson's advice, but go with your gut feeling and don't buy or rent any boot that you are not convinced fits you. Ski boots can seem very constricting if you are not used to them. Make sure you spend enough time wearing them around the shop before committing yourself.

Size
■ Lean right back. Your toes should just skim the front of the boot. If they can't reach it the boot is too big; if your toes are pushing hard against the front, they will become very sore.
■ Kick first your heel, then your toe against the ground. Does your foot slide backwards and forwards? If it does, the boot is probably too big.

Control
■ Try to stand on tip-toes inside the boot. You shouldn't be able to raise your heel more than half a centimetre off the sole.
■ If you can roll your knee from side to side without rocking the boot, or if you can roll your foot within the boot, you will not have good edge control.

Comfort
■ Can you wiggle your toes? If not they will become cold and cramped.
■ Are there any points that become painful after you have worn the boots around the shop for a while? Vulnerable spots are your ankle bones (inside and outside), shins and toes.

ADJUSTMENTS AND FEATURES

The following options may be available only on the top boots in a manufacturer's range. They allow you to customize your boots to fit your skiing style. Before settling for a cheap boot it might be worth investigating whether one of these features would change your life. None of these features are generally required by beginners.

Canting adjustment
Knock-kneed or bow-legged skiers may find it hard to set their skis flat on the snow. A canting adjustment allows the sole of the boot to lie flat when you are in a neutral skiing position. You can tilt the cuff of the boot towards the inside or outside until you find the optimal position; once it is adjusted you do not have to alter the setting. An old fashioned way of achieving this was to use wedges, but unless you have a fairly pronounced geometry problem, the canting feature of a good pair of boots should be adequate.

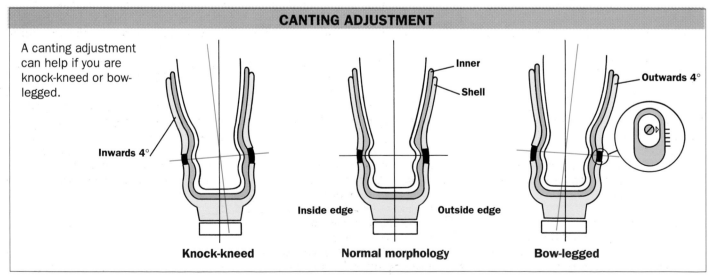

CANTING ADJUSTMENT

A canting adjustment can help if you are knock-kneed or bow-legged.

Inwards 4°

Inner
Shell

Inside edge   Outside edge

Outwards 4°

Knock-kneed   **Normal morphology**   **Bow-legged**

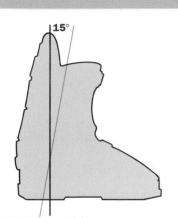

Upright position
Comfortable for those not used to ski boots. Good for beginners, and standing around.

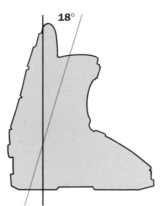

Medium lean
Ideal position for most types of skiers and skiing.

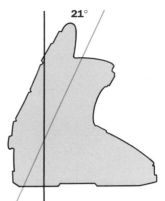

Extreme forward lean
Good for extremely aggressive skiers, but hard on the shins.

Forward lean adjustment
Forward lean is the angle between your shin and the vertical with the boot closed. On some advanced boots this can be adjusted between 15 and 20 dcgrccs. In the late seventies it was thought trendy to use maximum forward lean but, with modern skis, a less extreme position works better (and is easier on the shins). A forward lean adjustment allows you to experiment and find what works best for you.

Flex adjustment
Your boots' stiffness at the ankle can make a surprising differencc to your skiing. A softer flex results in smoother, more flowing skiing; a stiffer flex is more precise but less forgiving. With a stiffness adjustment you can alter this at will.

Sole height adjustment
Some ski boots boast an internal adjustable sole height. Raising your foot can remove surplus space without having to overtighten the boot. Lowering the sole gives better edge control (and colder feet). In practice, a good moulded footbed eliminates the need for this feature.

Power strap
A Velcro fastening around the boot cuff permits a more positive fit around your calves and gives better control.

Custom-moulded footbeds
Customized footbeds are strongly recommended for intermediate and advanced skiers. These are heated up and moulded to the shape of your feet. They then fit into any boots, stabilizing your feet and supporting your arches. The result is superior control, elimination of pressure points and reduced fatigue.

Boot surgery
There are a number of small modifications that can be made to a boot to improve comfort, such as adding or cutting out padding, increasing arch support or bending the shell. This is especially helpful for those with localized problems such as pressure points, bunions, pronounced ankle bones or odd-sized feet.

If you are buying boots, the shop should offer you free fitting sessions - after all, you are spending a lot of money. Don't be shy about asking for advice on adapting your boots.

Foam
If you are very unhappy with the fit of your boots and have tried other options, it may be worth having your inners foamed. Expanded polyurethane foam is injected under pressure into your boots as you wear them. It solidifies, taking the exact shape of your feet. Foaming offers unsurpassed control, but is expensive and must be carried out by an experienced technician.

TIPS
- Don't ski too hard in new boots: once you get a bruise, it's hard to relieve the pressure.
- Cut your toe-nails.
- Make sure your socks don't ruck.
- Don't overtighten your boots.
- Remove your inners at night if they seem wet.
- Never leave your boots in the car overnight or in an unheated room.
- Do the first few runs each day with your boots slightly looser than normal.
- Loosen your boots on chair lifts if necessary.
- Wear your boots around the house before your holiday.

PRETTY IN PINK
On average, women have a slightly different foot shape from men. Women's boots, however, are not usually performance models so, if you are an advanced skier, first see if you can use a general or men's model.

SKIS

The right pair of skis feels like part of your body. The wrong pair can seem viciously unco-operative. Take your time when selecting skis and, if in doubt, rent before you buy.

WHAT YOU WANT FROM YOUR SKIS

- Ease of turning.
- Equilibrium at speed.
- Grip on ice.
- Vibration absorption.
- Speed of running.
- Precision.
- Forgiveness of mistakes.
- Lightness.
- Image, colour and design.

SHAPE

Side-cut
The edges of your ski are not parallel: your ski is narrower in the middle or 'waist' than at the tip or tail; the tip is the widest point of the ski. This is of great importance when it comes to turning. The more pronounced the side-cut, the quicker and easier the ski will turn. The less side-cut, the faster and more stable the ski.

Camber
Your skis are arched so that if you put them unweighted on the snow, only the tip and tail are in contact with the surface. This camber helps to distribute your weight over the whole length of the ski. Without camber, your skis would be unstable, have poor grip on ice and provide poor feedback to you. Loss of camber is one of the signs that your skis are ready for the scrap heap.

Stiffness
A ski's stiffness can be measured in two directions: in simple bending, for instance under your weight, and in torsion (when the ski is on its edge, the forces tend to twist it about its axis).

Both bending and torsional stiffness vary along the length of the ski, producing the ski's characteristic handling and 'feel'. In general, a soft ski is easier to turn and more pleasant to use; the challenge for manufacturers is to combine this with the torsional stiffness necessary for precision and a good grip on ice.

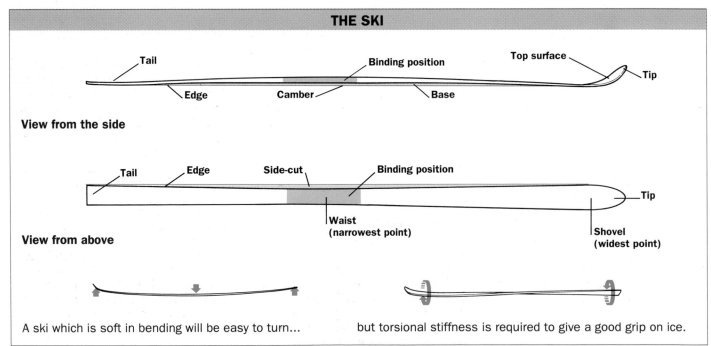

THE SKI

View from the side

Tail — Binding position — Top surface — Tip
Edge — Camber — Base

View from above

Tail — Edge — Side-cut — Binding position — Tip
Waist (narrowest point) — Shovel (widest point)

A ski which is soft in bending will be easy to turn... but torsional stiffness is required to give a good grip on ice.

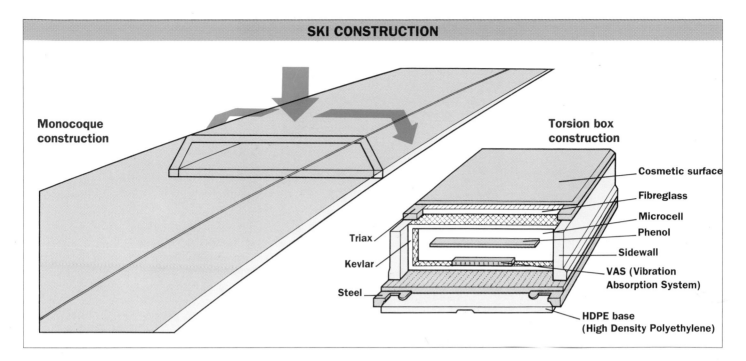

SKI CONSTRUCTION

Monocoque construction

Torsion box construction

Cosmetic surface
Fibreglass
Microcell
Phenol
Sidewall
VAS (Vibration Absorption System)
Triax
Kevlar
Steel
HDPE base (High Density Polyethylene)

CONSTRUCTION

Over the years, manufacturers have tried numerous ways of solving the technical challenges posed by ski construction. A number of different systems are used, many of which involve laminating or layering various materials. Alternatively, some manufacturers build their skis around a polyurethane foam core, or a carefully designed metal 'torsion box'. Most advanced is the monocoque design, in which the upper surface of the ski is not merely cosmetic but, by curving down to meet the edges, actually provides the ski's strength and stiffness.

Ski designers have always been quick to exploit new advances in material technology, both for performance and marketing reasons. Although wood is still used, it is usually as a 'filler' to keep the weight of the ski down. Aluminium or fibreglass are most commonly used to provide strength, although increasing numbers of skis include Kevlar, titanium, carbon or even boron fibres. As a general rule, the more exotic-sounding the material, the less of it is actually present and the more expensive your skis.

TYPES OF SKI

■ Slalom skis are stiff, with a pronounced side-cut. They are easy to turn, cope well with moguls, and offer good grip on the slopes. They can, however, be unforgiving and 'nervous' (unstable at speed). Slalom skis are rarely good in powder, due to the stiffness of their tips.

■ Giant-slalom (GS) skis are less stiff than slalom skis, and can be taken slightly longer. As a result they are smooth and powerful, good at higher speeds and in powder. GS skis or softer slalom skis are the main choice for advanced skiers.

■ Recreational skis are usually based on slalom or giant slalom designs, but are softened to allow easier turning and more forgiveness of mistakes. Though they're not the most stable skis at speed, they are appropriate for the majority of skiers.

■ Beginners' skis have limited side-cut in order to provide stability. For ease of turning they are soft and should be taken very short.

■ Mogul skis are usually based on slalom skis, although the stiffness and strength are occasionally enhanced.

■ Extreme skis are designed for steep slopes and gullies. They are similar in construction to mogul skis and come with built-in image, essential for armchair couloir skiers.

■ Women's skis have a softer flex at tip and tail for easy turning, though this gives them less stability at speed. The graphics are also modified, for those who require colour co-ordination.

■ Powder skis are broader than slalom skis, and fairly soft, especially in the tips. They are skied slightly shorter than usual. In Europe, it's hardly worth buying a pair yourself, though for wonderful powder you might want to rent for the day.

■ Compact skis were very popular in the mid-seventies, especially for low intermediates. They were broad, with almost no side-cut and sometimes with round tips. They tended to chatter at speed and were unreliable on ice. They are now all but extinct.

RENTAL SKIS

Good shops have a selection of skis to suit everyone's ability. This usually includes rental versions of beginners' or recreational skis, as well as top of the range models. Prices vary accordingly. Bindings on rental skis are mounted to allow for a wide variety of boot sizes.

RECOMMENDED SKI LENGTHS

Draw a straight line between your height (left scale) and the type of skiing you intend to do (right scale). Where this line crosses the central scale indicates the ideal length of ski for you. If you are particularly light for your height, drop down 5 cm. If you are particularly heavy or athletic, go up 5 cm.

In the example shown, a 1 m 75 (5ft 9in) skier would start off on a pair of 1 m 60 skis (A). She increases the length as she improves, via 1 m 75 as an intermediate (B), until she can ski parallel and uses a pair of 1 m 85's (C). As an advanced skier, she would choose a ski between 1 m 90 and 2 m, depending on the type of skiing she enjoys most (D and E).

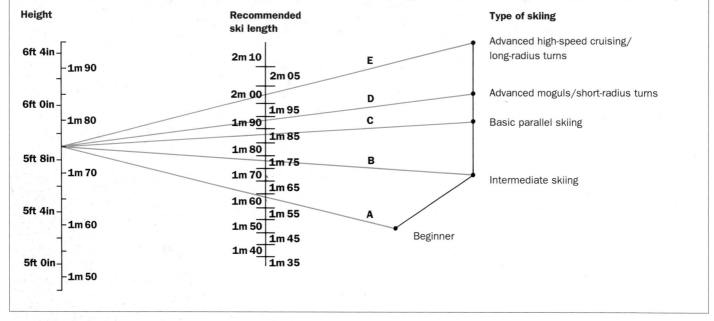

LENGTH

Once you have decided on the type of ski, you must choose the right length. Skis generally come in 5cm increments, although some manufacturers do intervening lengths, especially of useful sizes such as 1 m 97 and 2 m 03. Note that US manufacturers measure around the tip, not straight up, so their skis tend to be a couple of centimetres shorter than you expect.

The appropriate length of ski depends on your weight, height and skiing ability. The type of skiing you aim to do is also important. As a general guideline, skis should be your height plus 20cm. Some manufacturers have their own idiosyncratic grading systems, and you should follow their recommendations as far as you feel comfortable with them.

If you are a beginner you should start with a short ski, shorter than your height, which is easier to turn and manoeuvre. As soon as you begin to move at any real velocity, it's time to move up to a slightly longer ski, which will be more stable at speed. Take yourself up 5cm for each week of experience until you reach your correct ski length.

CONDITION

If you're renting skis or digging your own out of the attic at the beginning of the season, check them before use.

Shape

Look down the length of the skis to ensure that they're not warped. Squeeze the skis together to check their camber. The skis should touch at the tips and tails, and you should be able to press them together in the middle. They should immediately bounce back when released.

Bases

Run your hand over the surfaces. They should be smooth, with no gouges. If rental skis need waxing, the shop should do it without extra charge.

Edges

The edges must not be dislodged from the ski anywhere, no matter how slightly, and should be sharp. To check this, scrape a sliver off a finger-nail by pulling it across the edge.

MAINTENANCE

There is little point in investing in a good pair of skis if you do not keep the edges sharp and the bases flat and waxed. It is surprising how much a good ski service can improve your skiing. The simplest and safest way is to take your skis to a good shop once per week of skiing. In icy conditions this is especially important. Shops in ski resorts offer a convenient overnight service.

While most skiers prefer to leave ski maintenance to the professionals, it is not difficult to do it yourself, just messy and time-consuming. In any case it is worth knowing how it is done. You will need: a set of clamps to hold the ski, a small whetstone, a file, steel and plastic scrapers, a P-tex candle, wax and an old iron.

Bases

Using the steel scraper, smooth off the base, getting rid of any protruding scars. The surface should be flush to the edges. Fill gouges with polyethylene from a P-tex candle. Drip the P-tex into the gouge, then scrape off the surplus with the scraper to leave the base flush. A repair shop may be able to fill holes with a denser plastic, and can also patch more serious damage.

Edges

Use the whetstone to remove any burrs. This by itself may leave the edge sharp enough, otherwise use a special edge file. Competitors file their edges at various acute angles, but for most skiers 90 degrees is fine. Be careful to keep the edge flush with the base. Dull the edge about 15 cm back from the tip and tail using the stone. Advanced skiers and racers mark their right and left skis and keep the inner edge sharper than the outer.

Use a scraper to make sure your bases are smooth and flat.

Pull the file towards you in long strokes until any nicks on the edges are no longer visible.

Sharpen your edges by filing them at 90 degrees. A right-angle file is a handy tool.

Waxing

There is a variety of waxes for different temperatures and snow conditions, but a good universal wax will usually do. Make sure your skis are clean; if you've just sharpened your edges, remove any metal filings from the bases. Drip the wax onto the base in a long dotted line. Then iron evenly. Wait for the surface to cool and remove all the excess wax with the plastic scraper, so only a thin layer remains. Make sure the edges are clear of wax.

Use an old iron to wax your skis.

Care of your skis in transit and off season

If you carry your skis on a roof rack, always cover the bindings to protect them against salt and grit. Ski boxes hold several pairs and are a convenient alternative. Both boxes and lockable roof racks are rented by many ski shops.

If you are travelling by aeroplane, your skis should also be protected in a ski bag. While still at the destination airport, have a quick check to make sure that your skis have not been damaged en route.

Never leave your skis in their bag when you arrive home. Ideally, apply a heavy coat of wax to prevent the bases from drying out. Make sure the storage area is dry and cool. At the beginning of the next season, scrape off the wax, and check the bindings, edges and surfaces.

AVOIDING DAMAGE

A few basic precautions when you are skiing will help to keep your skis in good condition:
■ Be aware of the snow cover. Discolouration of the snow can indicate the presence of rocks close below the snow surface. If in doubt, keep your speed down.
■ Concentrate on the terrain ahead.
■ Turn on the fronts and tops, not the backs of moguls.
■ Don't ski across gritted areas.
■ If you can't avoid hitting a stone, take it down the length of the ski, rather than across it, which may pull out an edge and cause serious damage.
■ Don't worry too much. Skis are for skiing on.

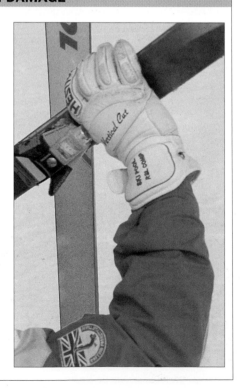

If you hit a rock, use the edge of the other ski to smooth any gouges in your bases.

CAR HIGHER

If your accommodation is far from the slopes, or you plan to visit nearby ski areas, driving may make sense. But mountains can be inhospitable places for cars, with low temperatures, corrosive salt and poor driving conditions. They can also be inhospitable for drivers, unless you enjoy shovelling snow and putting on chains. Before setting off, make sure your car is prepared: antifreeze and wiper fluid must be capable of withstanding at least -20°C (-4°F), and you should use a good quality winter oil. In addition, don't forget the following:
■ Green Card/proof of insurance.
■ Vehicle registration document.
■ Chains.
■ Light bulbs.
■ Warning triangle.
■ First aid kit.
■ Driving licence.

BINDINGS

In terms of safety, bindings are the most important piece of your equipment. They need to hold the foot firmly to the ski, and yet be sensitive enough to release should a fall put excessive strain on your leg. They also need to retain sufficient elasticity to pull your boot back to the centre of the ski in the event of a near-release.

If you choose to buy skis, it is worth buying good bindings, even as a beginner, since safety is crucial, and you can always remount the bindings onto new skis. New bindings should be mounted – free – when they are bought. Older bindings should be checked by a qualified technician at the beginning of each season.

THE PARTS OF A BINDING

Most makes of binding consist of three components: a heel-piece, a toe-piece and a brake. Sometimes the heel and toe are mounted separately, sometimes they are attached on one plate.

Heel-piece
This releases upwards, opening in a forward fall. Some models offer a diagonal or sideways heel release.

Toe-piece
This allows sideways release in the event of a twisting fall. A Teflon anti-friction pad under the toe allows the boot to slide easily even when your weight is pushing down on it during a heavy fall.

Brakes
When you step in to the binding, the brake lifts out of the snow. If your binding releases, the brake springs back down, preventing the ski from escaping down the mountain and causing injury to other skiers.

SETTINGS

Bindings are well designed, complex pieces of machinery, and need to be set correctly in order to offer a skier the maximum security. A premature binding release can be as dangerous as a binding that doesn't open.

Setting your bindings for your boots involves first adjusting the height of the toe-piece and the position of the heel-piece. The appropriate release settings can then be selected. The DIN (Deutsche Industrie Norm) scale is standardized across all makes of bindings. The appropriate setting depends on weight and level of skiing, ranging from one for a small child to 24 for a heavy, top-level competitor (see chart overleaf).

Front and rear bindings should be on the same number. Beginners ski on a looser setting, around two points less than more experienced skiers of equal weight. If in doubt, always get a qualified technician to set your bindings (and remember to take at least one boot with you to the shop!).

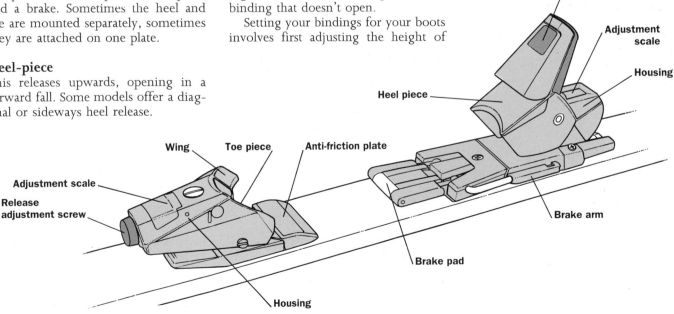

Heel piece · Binding release lever · Adjustment scale · Housing · Wing · Toe piece · Anti-friction plate · Adjustment scale · Release adjustment screw · Housing · Brake pad · Brake arm

A TYPICAL BINDING SETTINGS CHART

How to use the table:
1 Find the line corresponding to your height.
2 If your weight is on a higher line, move up to that row.
3 Find your level as a skier:
- If you are a beginner, stay on the same row.
- If you are an average or intermediate skier, move down one row.
- If you are an aggressive or expert skier, move down two rows.

4 If you are over 50, move up one row.
5 Locate your binding setting in the column corresponding to your boot sole length.

Caution: Make sure that you use the chart supplied with your own bindings.

SKIER MEASUREMENTS		BOOT SOLE LENGTH (mm)					
Height	Weight	<250	251–270	271–290	291–310	311–330	>330
	10–13 kilos (1st8lbs–2st1lb)	0.75					
	14–17 kilos (2st2lbs–2st10lbs)	1	1				
	18–21 kilos (2st11lbs–3st5lbs)	1.5	1.25				
	22–25 kilos (3st6lbs–4st)	1.75	1.5	1.5			
	26–30 kilos (4st1lb–4st10lbs)	2.25	2	1.75			
	31–35 kilos (4st11lbs–5st8lbs)	2.5	2.5	2	2		
	36–41 kilos (5st9lbs–6st7lbs)		3	2.5	2.5	2	
1m49 and under (4ft 10in)	42–48 kilos (6st8lbs–7st9lbs)		3.5	3	3	2.5	2.5
1m50 – 1m55 (4ft 11in – 5ft 1in)	49–57 kilos (7st10lbs–8st13lbs)		4.5	4	3.5	3	3
1m56 – 1m65 (5ft 2in – 5ft 5in)	58–66 kilos (9st–10st7lbs)			5	4.5	4	3.5
1m66 – 1m79 (5ft 6in – 5ft 10in)	67–78 kilos (10st8lbs–12st6lbs)			6	5.5	5	4.5
1m80 – 1m93 (5ft 11in – 6ft 4in)	79–94 kilos (12st7lbs–14st13lbs)			7	6.5	6	5.5
1m94 and over (6ft 5in)	95+ kilos (15st and over)				8	7	6.5
					10	9	8
							10

POLES

Ski poles consist of a shaft, a handle and a basket.

Length
To test the length of your pole, hold it upside down and grip it beneath the basket. Your forearm should be horizontal when you stand with your knees slightly flexed.

Handle
The most common is the strap type, with a loop of leather or webbing to attach the pole to your wrist. Almost all rental poles are of this type. The sword-grip type consists of a moulded guard which extends round the back of the hand. It is intended to make life easier, but in effect means that you have to trek back uphill to retrieve dropped poles after almost every fall.

Basket
For skiing on piste, the size of basket is irrelevant and many skiers prefer small baskets. In powder, a larger basket prevents the pole from sinking.

Shaft
This is usually made of aluminium, although composite materials offer an expensive and lighter alternative.

- Straight poles are cheap and adequate for most skiers.
- Corrective angles – a slight, forward bend below each handle – may help you to plant your pole correctly. A forward and a backward bend, on the other hand, cancel each other out and make little difference.
- Aerodynamic poles are important for downhill racers, speed skiers and show-offs.

Left to right: Sword-grip handle, standard pole, corrective angle pole, corrective angle racing pole for slalom and moguls.

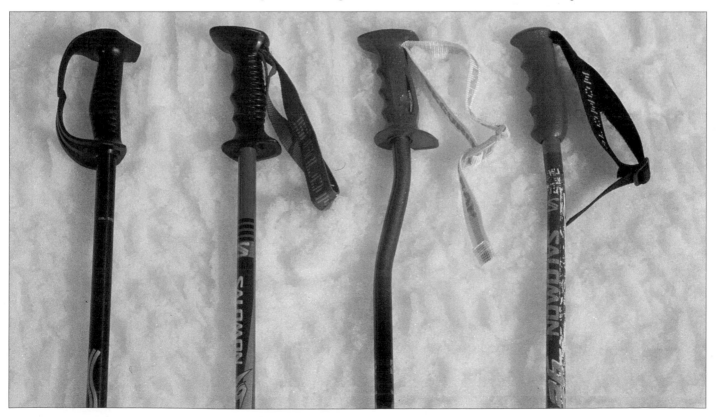

CLOTHING

Ski clothing must protect the skier in adverse weather conditions. It must be lightweight, breathable, water resistant and loose enough to permit unrestricted movement.

When considering your clothing requirements, remember to take into account the effects of moisture, wind chill, altitude and sun.

■ Moisture, whether caused by snow or sweat is at best uncomfortable, and at worst causes you to lose heat.

■ For every increase in wind speed, the wind chill factor increases the level of cold.

■ For every 1000m (3300ft) gained in altitude, the temperature drops by 6°C (11°F).

■ On the other hand, if the sun is shining all the physical exertion can make you very hot.

BODY CLOTHING

Ski clothing can either be a one-piece suit or a jacket and trousers. A one-piece is recommended for powder, otherwise jacket and trousers are more convenient. Any jacket must cover the kidney area. Trousers, also called salopettes if they come high above the waist, should have a high back to stop snow entering in a fall.

Clothing should not be of slippery material which will provide no braking in a fall, and it must be waterproof and windproof. Zips should be of plastic, as metal can freeze to the skin. They should have large toggles that can be adjusted without removing gloves. Sleeves should have cuffs with elastic or Velcro straps to prevent snow from entering. Trousers should fit over the ski boot.

WIND CHILL FACTOR				
AIR TEMPERATURE °C (°F)	EFFECTIVE TEMPERATURE °C (°F) Taking into account wind speed			
	8kph(5mph)	30kph(20mph)	50kph(30mph)	80kph(50mph)
0 (32)	-4 (25)	-14 (7)	-18 (0)	-20 (-4)
-8 (18)	-13 (9)	-25 (-13)	-31 (-24)	-33 (-27)
-16 (3)	-22 (-8)	-37 (-35)	-43 (-45)	-46 (-51)
-24 (-11)	-31 (-24)	-48 (-54)	-56 (-69)	-59 (-74)

The temperature falls rapidly as the wind speed increases.

THE LAYER EFFECT

When dressing for skiing, remember that three thin layers are more effective than one thick one.

Wicking layer
Preferably of polypropylene or cotton, this layer lies next to the skin and draws the moisture from the body outwards. It consists of a vest or T-shirt and long johns or woolly tights.

Pile layer
This adds bulk, which traps air and insulates you from the cold. It could be a fleece or woollen sweater, perhaps supplemented with a thick shirt.

Outer shell
This should be water and windproof but, rather than trap water vapour, it should permit sweat to escape. It should include a decent hood for emergencies.

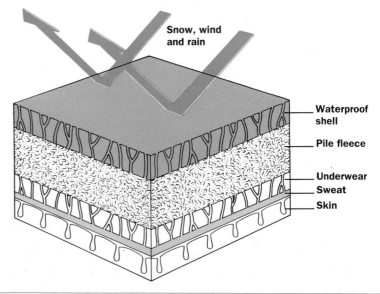

Snow, wind and rain

Waterproof shell

Pile fleece

Underwear
Sweat
Skin

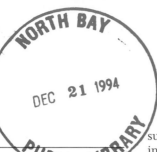
EXTREMITIES

Keeping your extremities warm and dry is very important (see chapter 19, see page 213).

Gloves/mittens

Water resistant gloves are crucial, especially for beginners, who tend to spend time digging around in the snow. They should be made of Gore-Tex or leather, and have a zip or Velcro tightener at the cuff to keep snow out. Mittens are warmer than gloves but clumsier.

Socks

Only one pair of socks should be worn, since two pairs can obstruct circulation or cause blisters. They should not be too thick, and should be of woollen towelling. They must not ruck and cause uncomfortable creases, and must come higher than your boot cuff.

Hats

A good hat covers the forehead and ears. To be on the safe side, carry a hat even in good weather (the ideal hat can be put in the pocket and forgotten until it is needed). A head band may suffice in warmer weather.

Scarf

A short scarf is useful to close the gap between jacket and hat. In extreme cold it can be used over the face if necessary.

Balaclava/face mask

A balaclava may be used for extremely low-temperature skiing, or for cold children. It is not, however, usually needed, and tends to become horribly soggy. A slightly more palatable alternative is a neoprene face mask.

ACCESSORIES

Skin care

Wind, sun and reflected glare are tough on the skin and you should never ski without adequate protection. Make sure that you cover all exposed areas, including your ears and any bald patches. Use sun cream with a sufficiently high blocking factor for your skin type. If in doubt use a total block cream. Reapply at intervals, and use a good lipsalve. After-sun cream can be a relief if you are over-exposed, but it cannot repair the damage done.

Eye-wear

You should never ski without adequate protection for your eyes, even on overcast days. Excessive exposure to ultraviolet light can cause snowblindness, which may result in permanent damage to your eyes. The best solution is to choose a quality pair of sunglasses. Retaining elastic and glacier blinkers are matters of personal preference.

Goggles are preferable when visibility is poor and for powder or serious bumps skiing. The strap should be worn over the hat. Wraparound eye screens are good for beginners since they are easy to clean after a fall. If you wear prescription glasses, look for special goggles and sunglasses that can accommodate them.

Rucksack or bum-bag

This is useful to carry the sandwiches, camera, skin cream, hat, etc. A rucksack should have a waist-strap to keep it in place over bumps. It can be a hassle on chair lifts, and care should be taken to avoid becoming entangled.

Ski-pass holder

The most basic version consists of a length of elastic or string around the neck, which is safe but irritating to take out all the time. A spring-loaded clip or a see-through holder on the arm are other possibilities.

Après-ski clothing

This, of course, depends on the type of holiday and resort. As a basic minimum you should pack a pair of non-slip boots and some warm casual clothes.

TAKE IT OR LEAVE IT

Nothing is more annoying than starting your skiing holiday by shelling out for a new pair of sunglasses because you left yours at home. Make sure you pack the following items:

- Skis and poles.
- Boots.
- Powder straps.
- Ski suit/jacket and trousers.
- Fleece/jumper.
- Socks, underwear, vests, long johns, shirts.
- Gloves, hat, scarf, headband.
- Sunglasses and goggles.
- Sun protection cream, lipsalve, total block cream.
- Bum bag and/or rucksack.
- Après-ski boots and clothes.
- Photos for lift pass.
- Swimsuit.
- Reading material (including this book!).
- First aid kit.
- Toiletry items.
- Passport.
- Travel documents (tickets, etc).
- Credit cards.
- Eurocheques/travellers' cheques.
- Local currency.
- Insurance documents.

WIRED FOR SOUND

Personal stereos may be fun, but they prevent you from hearing approaching skiers. They also tend to be antisocial for your colleagues and painful to fall on.

5 · Ski School

Enrolling in a class is the quickest and safest way to learn to ski. Being together with other people of the same ability is a crucial confidence-builder: you are no longer the worst on the slope, only one of the worst.

Learning to Ski

CHOOSING A SKI SCHOOL

Many larger resorts offer more than one ski school. Independent or private schools may employ younger or less conventional instructors, though all should be fully qualified. Your ski instructor's qualification is your only guarantee of quality and safety.

Qualification is supervised by national organizations, such as the Ecole de Ski Français (ESF), British Association of Ski Instructors (BASI) or Professional Ski Instructors of America (PSIA), as well as by the International Ski Instructors' Association (ISIA). Qualification is a highly selective process, involving courses in ski technique, teaching methods and safety. If you are on an organized holiday, your tour company may have a special deal with a local school. Check it out, but don't be bullied into accepting it.

WHEN TO TAKE LESSONS

Most schools run classes throughout the week, starting on Mondays, but this depends on the resort. You can also take single lessons.

Try to leave some time each day to work on your skiing outside the class. A good way to do this is to take lessons in the morning, when you are freshest, and to spend the afternoons going over at your own pace what you have learnt. Ski school is also a good way to meet people, and there may be someone in the class with whom you can practise after lessons. Another good way to improve is to ski with a group of more advanced friends, though be careful of well-meaning but incorrect advice, and don't over-stretch your ability.

Don't be too proud to return to school once you are a competent skier. A couple of important tips can improve your skiing dramatically.

THE CLASS SYSTEM

All ski schools use a numbering or lettering system, such as A for beginners, F for experts, etc. The ski school will probably decide for you which class you should join, either on the basis of the number of times you've been skiing or by asking you to perform a short test (though not if you're a complete beginner). In larger European resorts, schools offer classes of each level in several languages.

If asked to describe your skiing, there's no point in claiming you can do what you can't, or in being falsely modest about what you have already mastered. Don't be afraid to ask to be moved up or down after a day or so, if you feel you are not in the right class. The instructor may do it for you.

POTENTIAL PROBLEMS

Remember that you have rights as a customer and, though you may feel at a great disadvantage because of your ignorance of the sport and your lack of competence on skis, you are paying for a service. If you were promised an English-speaking instructor and you don't get one, insist.

A more serious problem is that if the class is too large, you will not only spend most of the time standing around waiting for the rest of the class to do their moves, but you may be so far away from the instructor that you end up imitating the mistakes of the pupil in front of you. Obviously an important tip here is to try to stick right behind the teacher, but there could be a lot of competition for this position (good teachers make sure that everyone gets some time at the front of the class). If you are becoming frustrated, don't hesitate to complain to the school. They should either move you or supply another instructor and split the class.

PLEASE SIR...

Before you sign up for classes, make sure you ask the following questions:
- What is the guaranteed maximum class size?
- In which language will the instruction be?
- What will I be learning?
- Can I change classes if I am too good/bad?
- Where will we be skiing?
- What kind of ski pass should I buy?
- Where do we meet?
- How do I recognize my teacher?
- Are any extras, such as video, included?

EXTRA OPTIONS

Some schools offer extras, such as races on the last day, or a video lesson followed by a session in the bar later on to replay and criticize. Races can be good fun, and stretch your abilities. Video is useful in identifying major stylistic flaws, especially for intermediates or advanced skiers who may have unsuspected, ingrained faults.

PRIVATE LESSONS

Although daily lessons are essential for beginners, their necessity decreases with subsequent holidays. After the second or third holiday, it may make more sense to take the occasional private lesson, instead of signing up for a full week at ski school. The advantage of private lessons is that the instructor can concentrate on your individual needs, taking the time to diagnose where you need help and making sure that you understand any new concepts. You don't spend any time waiting for the rest of the class.

Even an hour or two of private tuition can give you lots of ideas on how to improve, which you can then practise on your own. This is particularly useful for those who have reached a plateau and don't quite know how to progress. Gather a small group of friends or family who are at the same level to cut the cost of a private lesson, and it could be one of your best skiing investments.

SKI TESTS

Most national ski organizations run a series of formal tests in which you may like to participate, either to evaluate your skiing progress, or simply for fun. The Ski Club of Great Britain, for instance, was one of the earliest to introduce tests in the 1920s. The Ecole de Ski Français system starts with the *flocon* (snowflake) for toddlers, and leads through the *étoile* (star) on to the *chamois* (mountain goat) and *flèche* (arrow) awards for children and equivalent grades for adults.

INTERNATIONAL DIFFERENCES

In the 1950s, there were marked differences between national ski schools, when French and Austrian ski instructors taught their own particular styles. Now, however, techniques have largely converged, and teaching methods are fairly uniform, especially for beginners.

Advanced skiers will still notice some national differences. The French tend to emphasize competition, rather than recreational skiing; slalom racing is compulsory for instructors and usual for advanced pupils. The Austrians still concentrate on style, the Americans enjoyment. However, in the final analysis, it is the teaching ability of your individual instructor that counts.

GLM AND *SKI ÉVOLUTIF*

The idea of learning to ski on short skis was developed in the United States in the 1960s by Cliff Taylor, and imported to Les Arcs in 1970 by Martin Puchtler and Robert Blanc. Known as the Graduated Length Method (GLM) in the States, and *ski évolutif* in France, you start on 1m skis, then graduate to 1m 35 after a couple of days. Progressing a few centimetres at a time, you end the one-week course on 1m 60.

Using these methods, you can skip snowploughing and stem turning and leap straight to the parallel level. On the positive side, it's good fun and you can make quick progress. On the negative side, you miss out on snowplough and stem turns, which play an important part in the learning process and provide an essential fallback in poor conditions. It is also hard to follow the GLM or *ski évolutif* in a resort that isn't geared to its specific needs: your rental shop needs a full stock of skis in all the different lengths, and a willingness to exchange equipment every few days.

The best solution is to adopt a modified form of the method, whereby you start on fairly short skis (though not as short as 1m, see page 42), and promote yourself by 5cm each week.

6 · CHILDREN

Skiing need not stop when the children are born. Children love snow,
and a skiing holiday can be a memorable family experience.
Make sure that your children are warm, and that it's fun to ski,
and you should all enjoy your holiday.

Skiing en Famille

WHEN CAN THEY START?

There is no reason why children should not start skiing as soon as they can walk properly, say around three years old. In some resorts they can even attend ski school at this age. However, before the age of seven or eight, most children do not master any advanced techniques, so they will not have missed out if they start a few years later. Be guided by the child: if he or she wants to ski, fine; if not, don't force it.

WHAT SHOULD YOU DO WITH BABY?

Very young babies should not be taken on the upper slopes because their inner ear cannot yet properly adjust to changes in pressure. Skiing with a slightly older baby on your back can be fun, but brings with it an element of risk. You must be an expert skier, and mustn't mind sticking to easy runs. It is not recommended in very cold weather or if the slopes are crowded.

Some resorts have a municipal crèche where you may be able to place your child. Otherwise try a local nanny: phone the Tourist Office before you arrive. The simplest and most satisfactory option may be to book a chalet holiday with a specialized tour group which offers an in-house crèche. Failing all this, you may have to take your own babysitter. Grandparents could be considered since they are cheap and usually no longer so keen on skiing as their offspring.

(See page 216 for information on skiing while pregnant).

WHERE SHOULD YOU GO?

Not all resorts are recommended for those with young children. But some, such as Flaine in France or Okemo in Vermont U.S.A., specialize in family holidays, offering crèches for infants and lessons for young children. Some resorts, such as Les Arcs, in France, offer free passes for children under seven years; some offer a 10% reduction for large families of three children or more.

Enquire before you book. Skiing with the family can be an expensive business, so self-catering and self-drive should be considered.

Leave the pram at home and take a frame back-pack if going to a snow-covered resort.

EQUIPMENT

Children feel extremes of temperature more severely than adults. In case of doubt, they should be dressed too warmly, rather than risk exposure. Gloves, hats and goggles should be attached to small children who might otherwise lose them. A crash helmet is advisable for little speeders. Children are especially vulnerable to sunburn, so make sure that they are adequately protected. Sunglasses or goggles may be too large at first, but eye protection is vital.

For infants, skis are made of light-weight plastic, with no sharp edges and plastic loops for bindings. They often have fish scales on the base, to prevent sliding backwards. They are worn with normal 'après-ski' boots, but are only for real toddlers as no technical progress can be made on them. Poles have a 'sword-grip' handle, since a loop is too fussy. Needless to say, boots should be comfortable and warm. Sometimes it may be difficult to find ski boots that are small enough.

Children's skis are shorter, softer versions of adult skis. Initial length should be around shoulder height. Unless the child skis several weeks a year, it is advisable to rent while the child is growing. Alternatively, invest in an economy model, but make sure that the bindings are of sufficiently high quality.

Champions start young.

Drag lifts shouldn't present a problem, though a helping hand may be needed on chair lifts.

SKI SCHOOL

French ski schools accept children from around three years old, Swiss ones in general from four years old. Most good resorts have 'snow gardens' for very young children. Ring the local tourist office before you book your holiday.

In France, children's instruction is very standardized and quite good. All schools follow the same levels, starting in the *nounours* (teddy bear) class, which is the lowest rung, for toddlers. Usually this is in a little fenced-off compound close to the village, at the foot of the lifts, easily recognizable by the profusion of penguins and elephants. Teaching is through games aimed at making children feel happy both on the snow and on their skis. They then progress through *flocon* (snowflake) class, in which they will learn snowplough turns, simple step turns and easy downhill runs, to the various *étoile* (star) levels, when they begin to compete.

Most teaching methods for children involve little explanation and a great deal of copying movements. This is all disguised as fun, games and, for older children, races. Children's technique often develops directly from the snowplough to parallel turns simply through progressive increase in speed and narrowing of the skis, much to the irritation and pride of the parents.

OLDER CHILDREN

As children grow, they soon become more adventurous skiers. This presents parents with a difficult problem: how to allow the child enjoyable skiing without excessive risk.

Trying to ensure your child's safety by forbidding certain things (such as jumping or skiing fast) is unlikely to succeed and is not in the child's interest in the long term. It is far preferable that children develop their own understanding of the risks of skiing and the ability to make responsible decisions for themselves. However, a ban on off-piste skiing without adult supervision should be enforced.

Nobody should ski alone; you should help your older children to find a group with which they enjoy skiing. The ski school is a good place to start, or you may be able to share the cost of a private instructor with the parents of your children's friends. If your children want to go off in a group, make sure that they have a piste map, that they understand when they have to return, and that they take an appropriate telephone number and some money in case of problems.

Children practise manoeuvring through poles. In the background, cartoon animals inhabit the snow garden for younger children.

7 · GETTING STARTED

The long-awaited moment has arrived: it is time to go skiing. This chapter takes you through the first few days, from picking your skis up at the rental shop, through your first moments on the snow, to negotiating your first slope. Your aims during your first few days should be:

- Gaining familiarity with your equipment and environment.
- Feeling comfortable standing and sliding on snow.
- Learning a comfortable, effective stance on skis.
- Developing a basic understanding of how to apply your edges.

CARRYING YOUR SKIS

Whenever you carry your skis, you should lock them together. Place the skis with running surfaces touching. Slide them against each other until the brakes interlock. On longer trips or, for instance, when loading your skis onto a bus, secure your skis together with a rubber or Velcro strap.

In narrow or crowded spaces, carry your skis vertically to avoid doing any damage. Carry your skis on your shoulder only out in the open. Before lifting your skis, check behind you. Then place them flat on your shoulder with the tips forward and down (this keeps the tails up high and out of mischief). The front bindings should be just behind your shoulder, to prevent the skis from slipping forwards. Never turn around quickly, and look behind you before putting your skis down.

Carrying skis may at first feel awkward and uncomfortable. But rest assured: you will get used to it!

Ski brakes serve a dual purpose: they prevent runaway skis and also hold your skis together.

Carry your skis with the tips down to avoid injuring bystanders.

PUTTING ON YOUR SKIS

On a flat surface

■ Lay the skis flat on the snow, side by side. For most skiers, left and right skis are interchangeable.
■ Plant your poles upright in the snow on either side of the skis.
■ Make sure there is no snow in your bindings.
■ Clean all the snow from under your boot, either by scraping the sole or by slapping the side of your boot with your pole. Use the other pole for support.
■ Step into the binding, toe first. Make sure your boot is seated in the front binding before pushing down on your heel. The heel binding should close with a satisfying click. If it doesn't, chances are it hasn't closed properly. Take your boot out and make sure there is no snow on it. (This description is valid for all step-in bindings. Should you somehow have got your hands on a different type of binding, probably a museum piece, learn how it works before getting onto the snow. Then follow the same steps, closing the rear binding in the appropriate way.)

On a slope

■ Place both skis carefully across the slope. If they show any tendency to slide down the hill, push them into the snow so they sit on a slight platform.
■ Put on the downhill ski first. Follow the same procedure as above, making sure that the bindings and boots are free of snow. Use your poles for support.
■ In order to click the rear binding closed, push directly into the mountain, not vertically downwards.
■ Repeat for the uphill ski.

Make sure that the sole of your boot is free from snow before putting on your skis: it could stop your binding from closing properly. *A sharp slap with a pole should do the trick.*

Position the toe of your boot carefully in the front binding before pushing down on your heel.

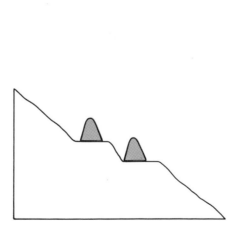

Push your skis into the snow to create a slight platform so you can put your skis on in comfort.

Uphill ski

Slope

Downhill ski

Terminology: uphill and downhill skis.

TAKING OFF YOUR SKIS

Almost all bindings are released by pushing down on a lever at the rear of the heel binding. At first you may feel more comfortable doing this with a pole, but there is a quicker way: simply step hard on one rear binding with the other ski. Then release the second binding in the same way with your boot. This requires a little balance, but you will soon master it. Racers have finely waxed and sharpened skis, so they usually bend down to open their bindings, but it won't harm your skis to release them in this way.

HOLDING YOUR POLES

In order to hold your pole, pass your hand up through the loop from below, then grasp the handle along with the strap. The strap helps to support your hand during pole plants, and in the event of a fall, the pole drops harmlessly away from your hand.

You should nearly always use your pole straps. The only exceptions are when skiing through trees or on plastic slopes, where it is preferable to climb back for an entangled pole than to dislocate a shoulder.

WHERE TO BEGIN

Most resorts have at least one very shallow slope ending in a large, flat area where you can start in safety. At this point, it is definitely worth having an instructor to explain things to you, keep an eye on you and select an appropriate spot for your first efforts.

Be wary of accepting help from friends who can already ski: the chances are that they have forgotten just how frightening even a shallow slope can look. Above all, don't just go to the top of a slope and put your skis on.

Stepping on the rear binding is a quick and easy way of releasing it.

Opening your binding using your pole.

Get used to holding your pole by passing your hand up through the loop: it's the safest way.

Pre-ski Warm Up

It's a familiar experience for every skier: you wake up and your body feels like it has spent the night in a tumble drier. Every muscle is tight; you have lost the ability to touch your toes or move your head; odd muscles, which you never thought you used in skiing, are sore.

The main culprit is the build-up in the muscles of lactic acid, a by-product of muscular exertion. The fitter you are, the more effectively it is eliminated. During the first few days of a skiing holiday, the unaccustomed exercise, combined with the effects of altitude on your cardiovascular system, causes the acid to build up in your muscles. The effect is compounded by any bruises and sprains you get during your falls.

The warm-up described here will help you to make a strong start to the day. It is intended to stimulate the bloodflow to the most important muscle groups, warming them and preparing them for exercise. Almost all of these exercises can be done without removing your skis. The warm-up should take about five minutes, and can be varied to concentrate on those muscles that feel they need it most.

Warm up at the top of the first lift and repeat the programme (or parts of it) after any break in your skiing, such as a long lunch or a ride on a cold chair lift. After your warm-up, take your first run on a relatively easy slope to give your body a chance to loosen up, before you ask it to perform at its limits.

Shrugs (8)
Lift your shoulders to your ears.

Neck rolls (8)
Roll your head forwards and sideways (not backwards).

Arm rotations (8 each side)
Start gently, rotating your arm slowly through 360 degrees from the shoulder.

Waist/obliques (8 each side)
Stand with your legs apart, and slide your hand down your thigh towards the outside of your knee.

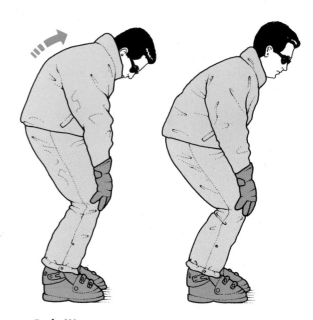

Back (8)
Stand with your legs slightly flexed, back rounded and hands on your knees. Lift your lower back, curling your upper back.

Shoulders (8)
Stand with your legs slightly flexed, back rounded and hands on your knees, and push each shoulder alternately towards the opposite foot.

Knee lifts (8 each side)
Lift your knee towards your chest.

Deep knee bends (8)
Flex down until your knees move through 45 degrees, then push back upright.

Abductors (8 each leg)
Keeping your leg straight, lift it to the side.

Leg raises (8 each leg)
Keeping your leg straight, lift it first forwards, then back. Don't swing it.

You don't have to take your skis off to do a quick warm-up.

Don't overdo it!

THE BASIC STANCE

THE KEY TO GOOD SKIING

A good stance is the foundation on which all later skiing skills are built – the key to getting your skis and your body to function as a harmonious whole. The basic stance is the ideal neutral position. It is how you should stand, and is the position to which you should always return. It allows you to:

- Place your weight naturally over the centre of the ski.
- Use subtle movements of your weight forwards and back as you control your turns.
- Use your legs under a calm upper body.
- Anticipate and respond to the demands of the terrain.
- Be relaxed and comfortable throughout a long day's skiing.

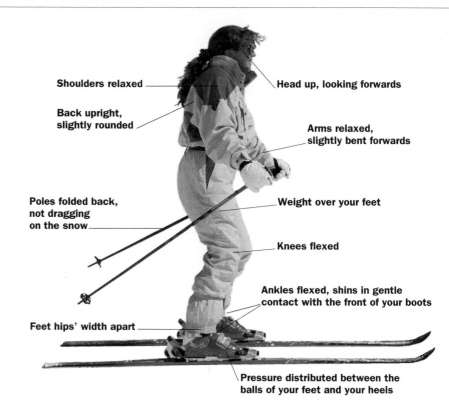

Shoulders relaxed

Back upright, slightly rounded

Poles folded back, not dragging on the snow

Feet hips' width apart

Head up, looking forwards

Arms relaxed, slightly bent forwards

Weight over your feet

Knees flexed

Ankles flexed, shins in gentle contact with the front of your boots

Pressure distributed between the balls of your feet and your heels

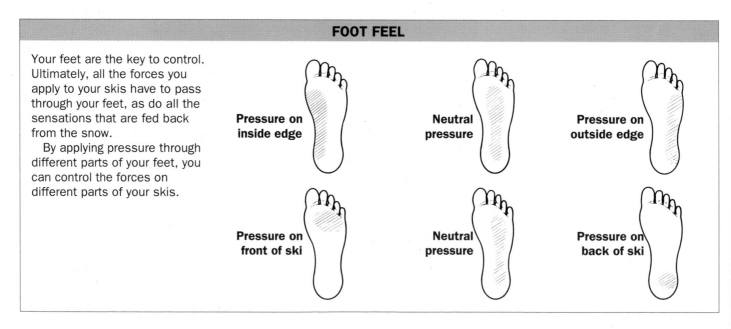

FOOT FEEL

Your feet are the key to control. Ultimately, all the forces you apply to your skis have to pass through your feet, as do all the sensations that are fed back from the snow.

By applying pressure through different parts of your feet, you can control the forces on different parts of your skis.

Pressure on inside edge

Neutral pressure

Pressure on outside edge

Pressure on front of ski

Neutral pressure

Pressure on back of ski

If your weight is too far back, your skis won't turn, and your thighs will tire quickly.

If you bend too much at the hips and waist, you can't use your legs for steering. Your back and shoulders will tire quickly.

TIP

■ Your basic stance must be stable and balanced: you should feel comfortable holding it indefinitely. If you don't, you may be too tense; try to relax!

EXERCISES

■ Get used to your basic stance. Rock forwards, feeling your weight moving over the balls of your feet until it pushes against your shins. Rock backwards until your weight is over your heels and pushes against your calves. Note how much support you receive from your boots. Which is the most comfortable position?

■ Experiment with different foot separations, finding the most stable and comfortable position.

■ Become aware of where the tips and tails on your skis are. Lift the tail of one ski, keeping the tip on the snow; then lift the tip, keeping the tail down. Keep your body in the basic stance throughout by balancing on the other ski.

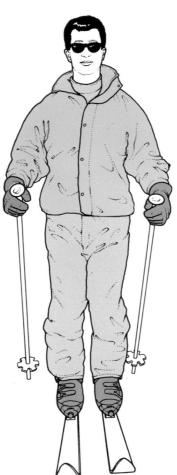

A closed stance is elegant ...

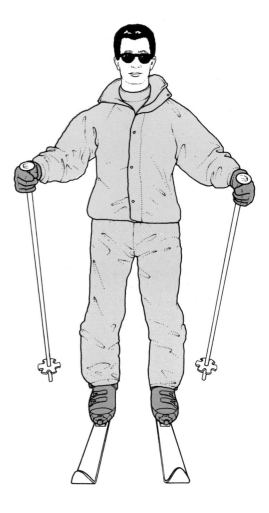

but an open stance is more stable and relaxed.

WALKING

TAKING YOUR FIRST STEPS

Using co-ordinated ski and pole movements, you can walk around on the flat. This is a good way to familiarize yourself with your skis.

TIPS

■ Use your poles for balance and to stop you sliding backwards. Your right hand goes forwards with your left leg.
■ Since your heels are held down, take small steps rather than large ones.

EXERCISE

■ Try walking on the flat without poles: this will force you to transfer your weight from leg to leg correctly.

Keep your skis on the snow and slide them forwards, one step at a time.

MAKING FRIENDS WITH YOUR SKIS

You have to learn to view your skis as an extension of your body. This might sound outrageous to you at this point, struggling with these absurd, plank-like appendages attached to your feet.

However, from carrying them in the streets without knocking anyone out with the tails, to knowing where your tips are under a thick layer of powder, getting to feel at home with your skis is an essential part of the learning process.

A speedier but more tiring way of moving around is to plant both your poles simultaneously and push yourself forwards.

The Fall Line

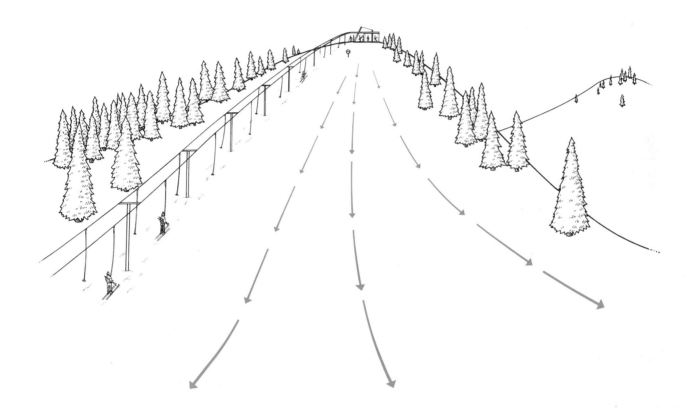

Initially, you may feel somewhat bewildered at the number of new things to learn. You have little time to take in your surroundings. Stop. There is something about the slope of which you absolutely must be aware: the fall line.

The fall line is the name given to the most direct line down the slope. It is the direction in which a ball would roll if you let it go. It is the direction in which gravity is pulling you. Point your skis at right angles across the fall line, and they will not slide. Point your skis down the fall line even a little, and

you are asking them to accelerate.

The fall line does not always describe a straight line: it shifts with any local change in the direction of the slope. You must be aware of these shifts, so that you can react to the direction in which gravity is pulling you.

Good skiers' awareness of the fall line is as keen as experienced sailors' awareness of the wind, with all its subtle shifts in direction. The sooner you build this awareness, the sooner you will be able to feel that you are in control of your skis, flowing with them instead of fighting them.

The fall line always describes the steepest line from any point. Its direction is not the same at all points on the slope, and it doesn't always follow a straight line.

THE NON-SLIP POSITION

FINDING YOUR EDGES

As a beginner, one of the first important lessons to learn is how to prevent yourself from slipping down the slope. Part of the answer lies in placing your skis exactly across the fall line (see page 67). This will stop them from trying to slide forwards or backwards. In addition, however, you have to use the edges of your skis.

If you allow your skis to lie flat on the snow, especially as the surface becomes steeper or the snow harder, they will tend to slip away from you. If, however, you rock them onto their uphill edges, their ability to grip the snow is increased, and they will not slip. Only when you have mastered this will you feel safe standing on a slope.

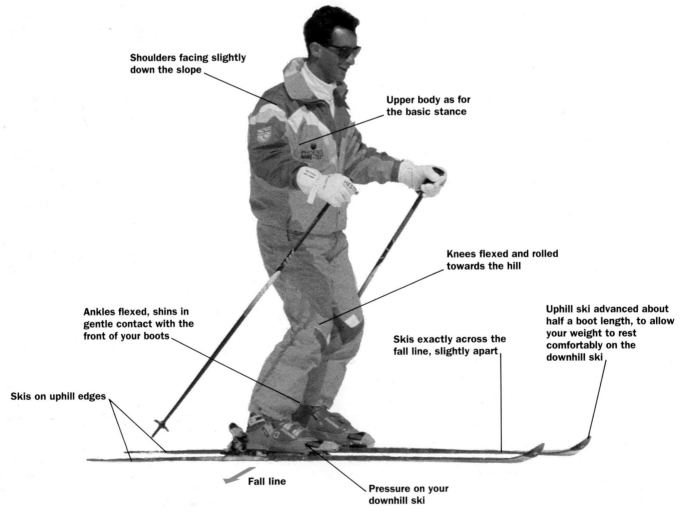

Shoulders facing slightly down the slope

Upper body as for the basic stance

Knees flexed and rolled towards the hill

Ankles flexed, shins in gentle contact with the front of your boots

Uphill ski advanced about half a boot length, to allow your weight to rest comfortably on the downhill ski

Skis exactly across the fall line, slightly apart

Skis on uphill edges

Fall line

Pressure on your downhill ski

SIDESTEPPING

CLIMBING A SLOPE

As a beginner you'll probably use side-stepping to climb up for your first short runs. Later, you will use it when manoeuvring. It is a good exercise, and familiarizes you with the use of your edges.

Keeping your skis parallel and across the fall line, step your way uphill, a shoulder's-width at a time.

1 Start in the non-slip position. Take a step with your uphill ski, keeping it parallel to the other one. Move your uphill pole out of the way and plant it further up the slope.

2 Transfer your weight to the uphill ski and lift your downhill ski.

3 Transfer your weight back onto your downhill ski. If you have kept your skis parallel throughout, you should be back in the non-slip position.

TIPS

■ Don't be too ambitious about the size of your steps. Keep them small to begin with.
■ Be aware at all times of where the fall line is. If your skis are not exactly across it, they will want to slide down the hill, either forwards or backwards.
■ Move the uphill pole up the slope before you trip over it.
■ Keep on your uphill edges by rolling your knees in towards the mountain. This will prevent you from slipping downhill.

THE STAR TURN

TURNING AROUND ON THE FLAT

The star turn allows you to turn around and face in a different direction. Step your skis around, 20 degrees at a time, until you are facing the way you want. It is not just a useful manoeuvre, but also helps you to become used to your skis. Practise the star turn on the flat, then try it on a slight slope, facing downhill. If you were to continue your turn through 360 degrees, the tracks in the snow would represent a star, hence the name.

TIPS

■ Make sure that you can turn both to the left and right, but if you are on a slight slope always turn facing downhill.
■ Move your poles as necessary to keep them out of the way and, on a slope, use them to prevent you sliding.

EXERCISE

■ Instead of pivoting your skis about their tips, try a tail-pivoted star turn. This is harder as you can't keep an eye on your tails.

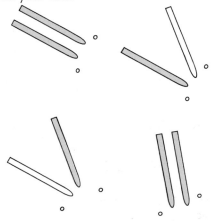

1 Plant your poles out of the way. Use them to prevent sliding if necessary.

2 Step one tail out 20 degrees, keeping the tip down.

3 Transfer your weight, and lift the second ski.

4 Bring your skis parallel, ready to take another step. Repeat until you are facing the way you want.

THE BULLFIGHTER TURN

TURNING AROUND ON A SLOPE

The bullfighter turn is similar to the star turn, but can be used on steeper slopes. This time, as you step around, pivot your skis alternately about the tip and tail, until they point down the fall line.

Once you have got a feel for your skis, the bullfighter turn is easy: you can turn in a few steps and you don't have to keep repositioning your poles. It should first be practised on the flat, then on a gentle slope.

KEY

Throughout this book you will find diagrams which tell you how your skis should be positioned and weighted in a particular manoeuvre. The following symbols are used:

Flat ski, unweighted

Flat ski, neutral pressure

Edged ski, gentle pressure

Edged ski, strong pressure

○   Pole plant

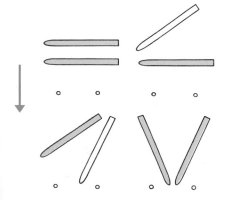

TIPS

- At first, use smaller steps.
- Take time planting your poles in the right place before you start.

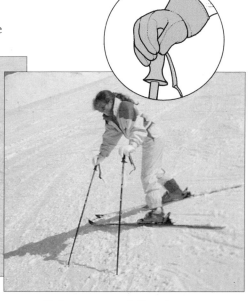

1 Start across the slope. Plant both poles downhill from your skis.

2 Step your uphill tail out 45 degrees, pivoting the ski about its tip.

3 Step your downhill ski into the fall line, tail to tail with the uphill ski.

4 Bring the uphill ski into the fall line. You should now be in a snowplough position facing downhill.

THE SCHUSS

LETTING YOURSELF SLIDE

Schussing means letting your skis run straight downhill. The term 'schuss' comes from the German word for a shot, which should describe your trajectory. Your goal should be to be able to schuss down the slope, relaxed and confident in your basic stance. In time, the schuss will be the fastest thing you can do on skis.

It is most important to choose an appropriate slope for your first attempts. Look for a gentle slope, with a natural run-out area at the end to help you to stop. Make sure it is clear of people, since at this stage the chances of your being able to stop or avoid obstacles are not high. Then enjoy the feeling of the wind in your hair.

1 Use the bullfighter turn to get into position with your skis pointing down the fall line.

2 Assume the basic stance and let yourself run. Look ahead and steer your skis gently with your feet to keep them parallel and pointing downhill.

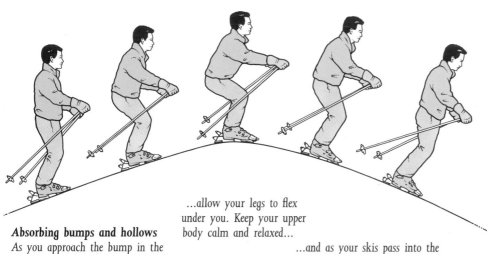

Absorbing bumps and hollows
As you approach the bump in the basic stance, relaxed, looking ahead...

...allow your legs to flex under you. Keep your upper body calm and relaxed...

...and as your skis pass into the hollow, push back into the basic stance.

EXERCISES

Try the following exercises while schussing, to improve your stance, balance and ability to absorb bumps and dips.

■ **Stance**
Vary your body position as you schuss, leaning forwards and then back, flexing low and then standing tall, varying the width of your stance. In which position do you feel most comfortable? In which position is it easiest to steer? To absorb bumps?

■ **Relaxation**
Pick up a snowball or glove as you ski along; ask a friend to hold out a pole at shoulder height, and ski under it.

■ **Balance**
Lift each ski off the snow for a few seconds; do a little jump; ski a few runs without your poles.

3 Respond to bumps and dips in the terrain using your ankles, knees and hips. Keep your upper body calm and relaxed.

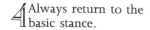

4 Always return to the basic stance.

Falling Over

LEARNING TO ACCEPT THE INEVITABLE

Falling is an inevitable part of skiing. There is no dishonour involved, and even good skiers fall over. It is one area in which beginners excel, because they generally have more practice than advanced skiers. Hurling yourself to the ground because you couldn't stop even used to be a recognized technique, known as the *arrêt Briançon!*

There are times when you really don't want to fall, such as when the slope is extremely icy or dangerous. In normal conditions, however, a fall is nothing to worry about, it can even loosen you up and show you that skiing needn't hurt! Learning when to take risks and when to play safe is an important part of mountain craft.

Even good skiers fall over.

TIPS TO AVOID INJURY

■ If you are falling sideways, try to keep your knees from hitting the snow first as this will tend to twist them. Land instead on your seat.

■ Don't fight the fall too hard. If you take a real high-speed crash, try to roll with it: swallow-diving into the snow can be more painful than expected.

■ Stop sliding as quickly as possible. Bring your legs below you so you can use your feet, with or without skis, to brake to a halt. Don't wear slippery clothes.

■ Never jam in your poles in front of you to stop. One of our most convincing childhood cautionary tales was about our mother who tried to brake by planting her pole against the trunk of a tree and broke her jaw on the handle. They reset it nicely though.

TERMINOLOGY

Falling is such an integral part of skiing that it has developed its own lore and vocabulary of euphemisms and nicknames.

Plant (As in head plant, shoulder plant, etc.) Driving of relevant piece of anatomy deep into the snow.

Three point yard sale (In extreme cases, five point, seven point, etc.) Generous distribution around the mountain of equipment - skis, poles, hat, gloves ... with an end result resembling a back-yard jumble sale.

Snow snakes Malicious but rarely seen reptiles living just below the surface of the snow. Responsible for many otherwise inexplicable falls.

Wipe out Adopted from surfing, this describes what happens when you are thrown off the frozen wave.

Pre-release A binding set too loosely or obstructed with snow will occasionally eject you unexpectedly, particularly in bumps or powder. This is the best excuse for a fall in which you lose a ski – impossible to refute without video evidence.

Catching an edge Letting a downhill or outside edge catch in the snow usually results in instant catastrophe.

WHAT A RELEASE

When you rent or buy skis, the shop is responsible for adjusting the bindings correctly. If, however, the bindings persistently release unnecessarily or, even worse, do not release when they should, they probably need readjustment. Unless you know exactly what you are doing, take your skis back to the shop.

Making your own adjustments is risky. If you do decide to try, tighten or loosen the release setting by only half a turn at a time, as the adjustment is sensitive (see page 45). If the problem persists, have the binding checked professionally.

Getting Up

BACK ON YOUR FEET

You've just fallen over and ground to a halt. Sit and recuperate for as long as you need, but be sure to let your companions know that you are not hurt. Then get up...

If your skis come off

Collect your skis. Check that the bindings are open, and then put your skis back on (see page 59).

TIPS

- Always put on your downhill ski first. If you lose only your downhill ski, turn around before putting on the lost ski.
- In powder it can be very hard to keep snow off the bindings. You may have to flatten an area in which to work.

If your skis stay on

Standing up on skis can be one of the greatest challenges at first. Yet once you have learnt the trick, it will be hard to understand why you ever found it difficult.

The first thing to do after any fall is to place your skis below you, across the fall line. You can either slide them round or roll over on your back (the dying beetle technique). Once your skis are below you, you are ready to stand up.

TIPS

- Make sure that your skis are exactly across the fall line before you begin straining to stand up.
- Plant your poles right next to your hips, to ensure adequate leverage.
- Get your weight forwards and over the skis using a short, sharp effort to gain some momentum to stand up.

In deep snow, cross your poles to prevent them from sinking in as you use them to stand up.

1 Sit just uphill from your skis.

2 Grasp both poles by the handles with one hand and just above the basket with the other. Plant them just behind your uphill hip.

3 Once in position, use a quick pull/push to shift yourself forwards and over your skis.

THE SNOWPLOUGH

LEARNING TO CONTROL YOUR SPEED

The snowplough offers speed control and a wide, stable position.

When you schuss down even a shallow slope, it is surprising how quickly you can pick up speed. The snowplough introduces the use of your edges on the move, using them to brake. It is reliable and stable, and even advanced skiers sometimes resort to the snowplough when they haven't got the space or energy to turn. First get a feel for the snowplough position when you're stationary, then try it on a gentle slope.

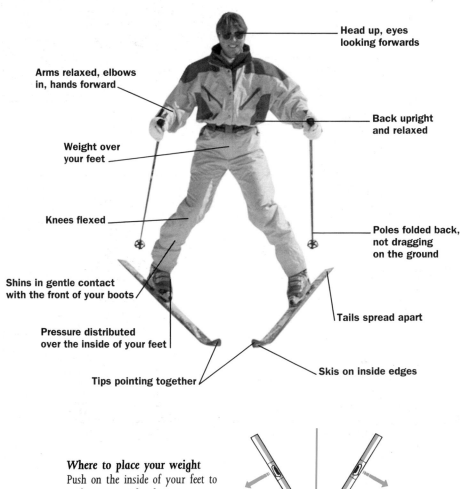

Arms relaxed, elbows in, hands forward

Head up, eyes looking forwards

Weight over your feet

Back upright and relaxed

Knees flexed

Poles folded back, not dragging on the ground

Shins in gentle contact with the front of your boots

Pressure distributed over the inside of your feet

Tails spread apart

Tips pointing together

Skis on inside edges

Leonard Bernstein fails to keep his tips apart.

Try snowploughing across the fall line. It is just like a normal snowplough, but with a little more pressure on the downhill ski, to keep you from turning downhill.

Where to place your weight
Push on the inside of your feet to apply your inside edges, counteracting the resistance of the snow. Use equal pressure on both skis.

GLIDING AND BRAKING SNOWPLOUGHS

The snowplough is a subtle tool, which can be used to apply varying amounts of braking. A gliding snowplough involves very little edge, just enough to prevent you from accelerating; in a braking snowplough you apply your inside edges strongly to slow yourself down. Experiment with the braking power at your disposal, varying the amount of snowplough you use and feeling the effect on your edges. How quickly can you stop from a schuss? How slowly can you go without stopping altogether?

TIPS

■ Keep equal pressure on both skis in order to run straight down the fall line.
■ To stop your skis from crossing, relax and use less edge. Compensate with a wider snowplough to achieve the same braking action.

Start off in a schuss in the basic stance.

Push out into a gliding plough.

Flex down and apply pressure on your inside edges strongly in a braking plough.

Rise up to release your edges and return to a gliding plough.

1 Start off in a schuss down the fall line in the basic stance.

2 Push out your heels into a gliding plough.

3 Increase your braking power by flexing at the ankles, knees and hips and pushing into a braking plough. Don't fold forwards from the waist.

4 Rise up to release your edges and return to the gliding plough.

8 · LIFTS

Ski lifts are your key to the mountains. Climbing uphill is laborious and time-consuming so the sooner you begin to use lifts, the more mileage you can cover and the quicker your skiing will progress. At first, they can be intimidating contraptions, but you will quickly master them.

DRAG LIFTS

The first lift you will encounter is likely to be a drag lift. The most common types are called button lifts or pomas, after their French inventor, the unlikely-sounding Pomagalski.

Drag lifts consist of a continuously moving wire, which carries a series of perches, shaped like plates. In the case of a button lift, these are mounted on a spring-loaded wire; in the case of a poma, on the end of poles. Perches may move continuously or collect at the bottom of the lift, waiting for the skier to activate a trigger. Either way, the goal is to place the plate between your legs and be dragged to the top of the slope.

GETTING ON

Hold your poles in one hand. Wait until it is clear to proceed. This may be signalled by an operator, a traffic light or a barrier.

Grasp the perch with your free hand. If there is a trigger to start your perch moving, make sure you trip it.

Place the perch between your legs, with your skis parallel and widely spaced.

Brace yourself to be pulled, but don't try to sit down!

Grasp the perch and trip the trigger.

CHILDREN OR VERY LIGHT ADULTS

On older lifts, children and very light adults may be lifted off the snow and rotated in the air for a few yards. The situation may be redeemable – 360 degrees though unnerving, may not be fatal; 90 degrees is. The only way to deal with this is to try to keep at least your ski tips on the snow and hope for a gentle landing. This phenomenon is mercifully rare and never happens on a nursery slope lift.

TRAVELLING

Assume a relaxed stance, keeping your skis parallel and allow the perch to pull you.

GETTING OFF

Keep an eye out for signs warning of approaching arrival.

As you reach the dismount sign, pull the perch out from between your legs with your free hand.

Release your perch, making sure that it does not hit anyone.

Clear the dismounting area immediately.

TIPS

■ There's a vicious jerk at the bottom of some lifts! If the skier in front of you gets yanked into the air, prepare for a jump start.

■ If the track dog-legs round a corner, be alert, keep your legs wide, relax and follow your perch.

■ Lift tracks occasionally slope downhill for a short distance. Hold your perch firmly, snowplough gently and don't overtake it.

■ If you fall over, clear the track quickly.

Take the time to appreciate your surroundings.

Leave your perch and get out of the way quickly.

T-BARS

As the name indicates, a T-bar consists of a large inverted 'T' which hangs by a wire from its stem. Victims line up in pairs; the lift operator pulls down the T as it passes, placing the stem between the two skiers and half of the T behind each backside. The pair are then pulled up side-by-side.

T-bars have been around for a long time, though most resorts are slowly phasing them out in favour of more user-friendly types of lift.

GETTING ON

Line up with your partner, poles in the outside hand.

As the operator places the T behind you, grasp hold of the stem.

TRAVELLING

Follow the track, keeping your skis parallel. Don't push your partner's boot or ski. Try and remember the other skier is your partner, not your opponent.

Turn to grasp the stem of the T.

Try to find a partner of similar height.

GETTING OFF

When approaching the end, decide which of you will hold the bar while the other disembarks: the skier furthest from the escape route should hold the bar.

Be careful when letting go of the T-bar: it can whip around and cause injury as the wire is sucked up into its holder.

Move away from the top of the lift as soon as possible.

TIPS

■ Find a partner with the same backside height as yourself.
■ If riding alone, or if you find you have to strain every muscle to stay on track, hold the end of the T under your outside buttock.
■ Lean in towards your partner's shoulder, and tell him/her to lean in too.

Let go of the T-bar carefully.

CHAIR LIFTS

Chair lifts provide a civilized way of getting up the mountain, offering a few minutes rest and time to admire the scenery. Chairs, usually two, three or four-seaters, mounted on a cable, move continuously up the slopes. The limousine version, high-speed quads, cruise up the mountain, but slow down considerably to pick up skiers.

GETTING ON

Hold your poles in your inside hand.

Spot the chair over your shoulder as it approaches. The unprincipled slide a few inches forward to let their companions' calves take the full impact of the chair.

Sit down as the chair reaches you. Ideally, avoid hitting your companions in the face with your ski poles.

Once the chair has left the platform, lower the protective bar.

Take care not to drop gloves, poles or litter. Should you lose something, note the number of the next pylon for orientation.

Hold your poles tidily as you sit down.

GETTING OFF

When you see the sign warning of arrival, open the protective bar.

If you're wearing a bum-bag or rucksack, make sure the straps are not snagged in the chair.

Raise the tips of your skis so they don't catch on the approaching dis-mounting platform.

As your skis touch the snow, stand up and push yourself off the chair with your free hand. Slide quickly out of the way to avoid being hit by the chair. Brake once you are well clear of your companions.

Ease yourself forwards and push off when your skis touch the snow.

Cable Cars, Funiculars, etc.

The first cable car was built in 1935 in Switzerland, while cog railways date from the last century. They provide straightforward ways of getting up the mountain, though some older installations can be painfully slow. No special techniques are needed, and those skilled in urban rush-hour techniques should feel quite at home.

A modern funicular speeds skiers to the summit.

OTHER TYPES OF LIFT

Outside the major resorts, you may encounter ancient and bizarre contraptions. In Italy there are still strange cages that you have to pursue down long platforms. In Eastern Europe you may be expected to bring your own grappling iron to clip onto the drag wires.

If you must ski in exotic locations, be prepared for these delights – and let someone else go first!

Individual cabins take skiers high above the Chamonix valley, in France.

MAKING THE MOST OF THE LIFT SYSTEM

THE SKI PASS

Often one or two beginners' lifts close to the village are free, otherwise you will have to purchase a pass. These are usually sold by area (for instance, one valley, or a whole resort) and by length of stay.

In general, beginners should not immediately invest in a full pass, since for the first couple of days they will not be taking advantage of the whole system. The shortest duration of pass is half a day. For ski passes longer than two days, a photograph is often required.

The pass must be shown on request and should be carried in an easily accessible place. Losing your pass is a disaster since it is expensive to replace and lift companies are rarely sympathetic.

Some resorts have points cards: lifts cost a certain number of points, which are punched out of the card by an attendant. Thus buying a booklet of twenty points could get you up a chair lift (6 points), a cable-car (10 points) and two drag lifts (2 points each).

QUEUEING

Queueing is a skill worth acquiring, especially in France or Italy. If the queue is not neat and well organized, choose your point of entry carefully. As you move forwards, the position of your shoulders is critical, though your progress can be consolidated by strategic use of poles and elbows. Remember that the bases, not the top surfaces, of your skis are sacrosanct, and that it is not good form to trample over other people's skis. Do not allow lifts to go up half-empty. If you become separated from your colleagues in a queue, wait for them at the top.

Queueing is an occupational hazard.

9 · THE BASICS

To feel in control of your skiing, you must be able
to determine your position on the slope, the direction
in which you are moving and your speed. To achieve this you
must learn to turn, and it is the feeling of
controlled speed and rhythm that results from linking turns
that makes skiing so exhilarating.

If you master the skills described in this chapter,
you will be able to descend a shallow slope in control and
get yourself out of difficult situations.

THE SNOWPLOUGH TURN

The snowplough turn (or wedge turn in North America) is the most straightforward of all turns. It is effective and reliable, and you'll see even experienced skiers use it when the visibility is poor, or when it's their turn to carry the picnic. It is initiated from the snowplough position by steering your skis into the fall line with your feet and legs. As you turn, the pressure you apply through your feet must move to your outside ski, just as the back seat passengers in a car are pushed against the door in a tight curve. To balance against this force, you must set your outside ski on a strong inside edge and push against it.

TO SNOWPLOUGH OR NOT TO SNOWPLOUGH

The goal for most skiers is to perform parallel turns in all terrains. You probably want to achieve this as soon as possible. Several teaching methods have been designed to avoid snowplough and stem turns altogether (for GLM and ski évolutif, see page 52). Some skiers find these helpful as they don't later have to unlearn a tendency to plough or stem their skis in turns.

Snowplough turns, however, are not a blind alley leading off the road to good parallel turns: they are a valuable step along the way. They teach the independent use of your skis, good edge control and steering with your outside foot and leg.

Given the choice between building towards good technical skiing and quickly learning an indifferent parallel turn, it is worth working on your snowplough turns.

Practise on a very shallow slope. Get a feel for steering your snowplough into the fall line and allowing the pressure to transfer to your outside ski. Make sure your upper body stays calm.

EXERCISES

■ Hold both poles out in front of you, with the baskets in one hand and handles in the other, to keep your upper body calm.
■ Tighten your turning radius by making a short slalom course out of ski poles. For a longer string of turns, force yourself to turn on a certain count. Start on ten, then reduce the time between turns by turning on nine, eight, seven...
■ Press both hands against your outside knee while you turn (see below). This helps you to apply pressure to your outside ski and use your edge correctly.

TIPS

■ Your skis know how to turn better than you do. Start the turn with gentle steering, the rest should follow.
■ Don't use your shoulders to start the turn: although you may force your skis around, the turn is hard to control and you risk over-rotating and ending up facing uphill.
■ At this stage, don't worry about planting your poles.
■ Learn to accept the frightening acceleration as you turn into the fall line. Don't lose your nerve.
■ Make sure you begin your turn before running out of room at the edge of the piste.
■ Try to get into a turning rhythm, starting each turn as you finish the last: rise and start, sink and finish; rise and start, sink and finish.

Practise exaggerated edging of your outside ski by pressing both hands against your outside knee.

1 Start in a gliding snowplough across the slope.

2 Steer your skis towards the fall line with your feet.

3 Sink slightly and allow the pressure to shift to your outside ski.

4 Push your outside knee forwards and into the turn.

5 Keep pushing against the outside ski until you come right out of the fall line.

6 As you finish your turn, rise back up into the gliding plough, before beginning the next turn.

TRAVERSING

USING THE CONTOURS OF THE SLOPE

Skiing across the slope, rather than directly down the fall line, is called traversing. Traversing is useful whenever you have to cut across the slope in order to reach a specific goal (such as a café). It is also a good way to control your speed: acceleration is greatest when you're pointing straight down the fall line, and least when you ski across it.

Until you can link your turns so that they flow into each other, they will be separated by traverses. You will spend a lot of time traversing, so it's worth getting comfortable in the correct stance.

Traversing is an invaluable technique so make sure you adopt the correct traverse stance.

Head up, eyes ahead

Shoulders relaxed, slightly angled towards the valley

Slight lean from the waist away from the mountain, to maintain balance over downhill ski

Poles folded back to keep them from dragging in the snow

Uphill foot advanced slightly to allow weight to fall on downhill ski

Skis parallel, on uphill edges to prevent them from slipping downhill

Ankles and knees flexed to absorb bumps and hollows, and rolled towards the slope

Fall Line

EXERCISES

■ Traverse with your uphill ski lifted slightly off the snow. Because your centre of mass has to be over your downhill ski, you have to exaggerate the lean out from the waist, teaching independent use of upper and lower body.

■ Practise traversing at varying speeds. For a slow traverse, point your skis almost across the hill. To speed up your traverse, choose a steeper line.

YOUR MOTOR MEMORY

The human body has a remarkable ability to learn movements, which it can then repeat even if the conscious mind is otherwise occupied. Just as you never forget how to ride a bicycle, so ski manoeuvres are stored in the motor memory of the brain.

The more frequently you can rehearse a movement in an environment that is free from stress and distraction, the more of a head start you can give yourself in the learning process. Throughout this book, if you come to a new and complex manoeuvre, don't wait until you are on the snow to try it: stand up and run through the moves a few times.

THE STEM TURN

STARTING TO FLOW

When you feel comfortable with your snowplough turns, allow your skis to come parallel between turns. This is less effort than staying in the snowplough position throughout, and allows you to master higher speeds.

Start in a parallel traverse, push into snowplough and turn as usual. As you finish your turn, let your skis come back together. Push out again into a snowplough to start the next turn. Try to get into a rhythm.

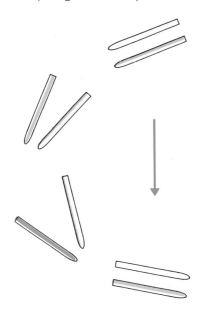

1 Begin in the standard traverse stance.

2 Push out into a snowplough and begin your turn.

3 Continue as for a snowplough turn.

4 When your turn is complete bring your skis parallel again in the standard traverse stance

Skills vs Techniques

Controlling your skis requires the development of three fundamental skills: steering, edging and controlling pressure. These are the actions that decide in which direction your skis point, the forces they experience from the snow and the path they follow. In order to apply these skills you also need good dynamic balance and the ability to choose an appropriate path.

The same skills – steering, edging, pressuring, dynamic balance and pathfinding – are used whether you are a beginner performing your first snowploughs or an Olympic racer. As you progress, however, the emphasis changes. For a beginner, the challenge lies in steering, as turns are started by steering, and all else follows. For advanced turns, steering becomes very subtle, and pressuring is the key to the effective use of your skis.

Most learning progressions, including the one described in this book, use a carefully designed sequence of techniques to aid the development of the fundamental skills. This has the virtue of breaking the acquisition of skills into manageable chunks and providing clear milestones.

Steering
You steer your skis by rotating them about this axis.

Edging
You apply your edges by rolling the ski about this axis.

Controlling pressure
You control the pressure on your edges by modifying the weight you apply to each part of your ski.

STEERING

There are two ways of steering your skis and usually you will use a combination of them.

Foot steering consists of turning your skis using just your lower leg. This is precise, but not particularly powerful. Use it for guiding your skis and making small adjustments to their path, for instance to keep your skis parallel in a schuss or at the beginning of a turn.

Using leg steering, you will rotate your thighs from the hip. It is much more powerful than foot steering, and can be used to steer your skis strongly, for instance to finish a turn.

Foot steering
Your knee remains stationary; only the foot and lower leg rotate.

Leg steering
Your entire leg rotates from the hip; your knee moves inwards.

EDGING

By varying the angle between your skis' base and the snow, you alter the amount of friction on the skis' edges.

In order to apply your edges, you must be able to move your knees from side to side over your skis. To do this you must maintain a flexed stance at your ankles, knees and hips. The rolling movement actually originates in your hips as you rotate your femur, pushing your thigh inwards. Try it first standing on the flat.

PRESSURE CONTROL

Pressure control consists of manipulating the force that you put on your ski during a turn. It involves taking advantage of centrifugal forces or dynamically modifying the pressure on your skis (for unweighting, see page 128). It also involves being able to control the exact point at which the forces act.

  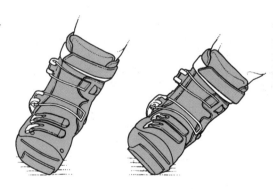

Flat ski **Slight edge** **Moderate edge** **Extreme edge**

DYNAMIC BALANCE AND PATHFINDING ABILITY

Good dynamic balance provides the crucial link between your skis and your body. Without it you will not be able to apply the appropriate steering, edging and pressure control. Pathfinding is the skill of choosing an appropriate route and reacting to the vagaries of the slope.

Your edges are sensitive instruments. You should be able to control carefully the amount of edge you apply, from none at all, right up to the maximum the snow will hold.

SIDESLIPPING

DEVELOPING CONTROL OF YOUR EDGES

Sideslipping consists of letting your skis slip down the fall line, controlling your speed by a careful use of the uphill edges. It introduces the use of parallel skis to brake.

You can use sideslipping to get yourself out of difficulty if you ever find yourself somewhere just too steep or too narrow. Never feel embarrassed if you need to sideslip. Even the most advanced skiers fall back on this technique when they run out of space to turn.

Sideslipping is an important skill, which will help you when it comes to controlling a skidding ski in a turn.

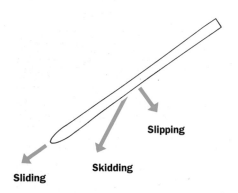

Your ski can slide straight ahead or slip sideways across the snow. Skidding is a combination of sliding and slipping.

Sideslipping is a controlled way of losing height.

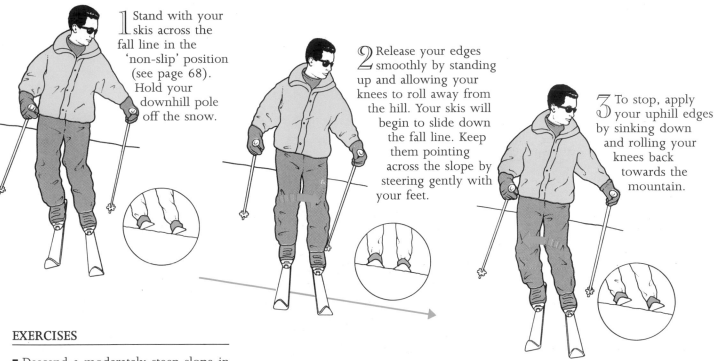

1 Stand with your skis across the fall line in the 'non-slip' position (see page 68). Hold your downhill pole off the snow.

2 Release your edges smoothly by standing up and allowing your knees to roll away from the hill. Your skis will begin to slide down the fall line. Keep them pointing across the slope by steering gently with your feet.

3 To stop, apply your uphill edges by sinking down and rolling your knees back towards the mountain.

EXERCISES

■ Descend a moderately steep slope in a series of short sideslips. Start with slow, smooth sideslips and work up to short, fast sideslips with aggressive stops. How quickly can you bring your sideslips to a halt?
■ Falling like a leaf (see right): forward and backward diagonal sideslipping. Steer your tips slightly down the fall line with your feet as you sideslip, and you will move forwards. Then steer your tips up the hill and begin to sideslip backwards. This is a good exercise to refine your edge and steering control.

TIPS

■ Sideslipping should be a very controlled move, like letting in the clutch on a car. Take your time and don't do anything sudden. Develop a feel for when your edges are losing their grip and starting to slip.
■ Keep the pressure on your downhill ski to ensure a smooth sideslip. Make sure also that your weight is distributed between your heel and the ball of your foot, or you will find it hard to keep your skis across the fall line.
■ Staying flexed throughout improves your balance and readiness to react to the terrain.

■ Look where you are going, not where your skis are pointing.
■ Always keep your skis slightly on their uphill edges. If their downhill edges catch, you will go over. Similarly, if you ski over your poles, it's curtains.

Falling like a leaf

Steer your tips slightly down the fall line to sideslip forwards. Then steer your tips slightly up the fall line to sideslip backwards. Practise falling like a leaf to improve your edge control.

THE KICK TURN

CHANGING DIRECTION ON THE SPOT

When you need to change direction but can't put in a real turn, you can use a kick turn. This is how to get out of a tricky situation if you run out of piste space. Practise kick turns in both directions before you really need them.

1 Stand with your skis parallel across the fall line. Plant your poles uphill, where they are out of the way but can be used for support.

2 Swing your downhill ski off the snow and place its tail on the snow next to the tip of the other ski.

3 Swing the ski back onto the snow, facing in the opposite direction. This position is uncomfortable and unstable so, as soon as it is back on the snow, transfer your weight on to it.

4 Bring the other ski round parallel.

5 You should now be standing in the original position, but facing the other way.

TIPS

■ Place your poles carefully before you start your kick turn. You don't want to have to replant them while you are teetering on the brink of disaster.

■ Replace the downhill ski exactly parallel. Otherwise, when you transfer your weight, you'll start to slide.

■ Lean back into the hill, not out over the valley, using your poles for support.

■ If you have knee problems, try to avoid kick turns.

Herringbone Climbing

A QUICKER WAY UP THE SLOPE

Herringbone climbing is considerably faster than sidestepping. The name comes from the track you leave. Start facing up the slope with your tips apart and your tails together. This puts your skis on their inside edges. Using your poles for support, step one ski at a time up the hill. Herringbone climbing is a little trickier than sidestepping, and can't be done on a very steep slope.

TIPS

■ It is your inside edges, not your poles, that should do most of the gripping. The steeper and icier the slope, the more edge you will need and the wider your V must be.
■ On steeper slopes, shift your grip on the poles to get better support.
■ Keep your poles planted away from your skis to avoid stepping on them.
■ Switch to sidestepping if the slope becomes too steep.
■ If you find herringbone climbing too frustrating, come back to practising it once you are more comfortable on your skis.

Step one ski at a time up the slope, using your poles for support. You should leave a neat 'herringbone' track.

10 · INTERMEDIATE SKIING

An intermediate skier is one who can confidently negotiate any slope of moderate difficulty, classed as a red run in Europe or a black diamond trail in the United States. You must be able to cope with steeper terrain, higher speeds and obstacles such as narrow pistes, bumps and hollows.

This chapter covers the techniques you will need in order to take advantage of the intermediate terrain of your resort.

THE BASIC SWING TURN

SKIDDING TO CONTROL SPEED

The basic swing turn is a natural progression from the snowplough and stem turns, enabling you to cope with higher speeds and steeper terrain. It is initiated in the same way, but the skis are brought together, or matched, during the turn. This allows you to complete the turn with a parallel skid, controlling your speed without the effort involved in a snowplough.

The name 'basic swing' covers a variety of turns, depending on the exact point at which the skis are matched. As you gain in familiarity, you will be able to introduce the parallel skid earlier and earlier.

In North America, basic swings are known as wedge or elementary christies (any turn that involves skidding is called a christie). Whatever the name, it is an extremely versatile turn: mastering the basic swing will give you the freedom of your ski area and lay the groundwork for parallel turns and more advanced ski techniques.

Many skiers progress naturally into the basic swing as they perform snowplough or stem turns with more speed. In a fast snowplough or stem turn, your inside ski is almost unweighted and flat on the snow. Allow it to drift in, parallel to your outside ski, and the result is a basic swing turn.

TIPS

■ The secret to matching your skis lies in allowing the pressure to transfer fully to the outside ski. If you are still encountering difficulties, try lifting your inside heel and pivoting the ski about its tip.

■ The skidded stage should feel similar to sideslipping: balance against the edges of your skis as they skid over the snow. This means allowing your skis to move to the outside of the turn, while your weight follows a shorter path. This is called angulation, of which more later (see page 126).

■ Avoid using your shoulders to initiate the turn. Start the turn by steering with your feet, and your skis will do all the work for you.

■ Don't worry about your poles. This form of basic swing does not have a sharp initiation, so a pole plant is not yet necessary.

■ As you gain in confidence, cut out the traverse between turns. Get into a rhythm: rise and plough, match and sink; rise and plough, match and sink.

EXERCISES

■ Can you lift your inside ski as you match and keep it off the snow until the turn is complete? This is the real test of whether you are transferring pressure effectively to the outside ski.

■ Match your skis earlier in the turn. Can you bring them together before they reach the fall line?

WHY DOES A SKIDDING SKI TURN?

Most skiers quickly acquire the knack of turning by letting their skis skid across the snow. It feels very natural. The reason is that the ski has been designed with this in mind.

Your skis' tips are wider than their tails. As a result, when they are put onto their edges and skidded across the snow, there is more friction at the tips than at the tails. They therefore tend to turn.

The radius of this turn can be controlled either by steering with the feet and legs, which physically twists the ski, or by moving your weight forwards or back. The further forward, the more friction on the tips of your skis as they skid, and the faster they turn. Try it.

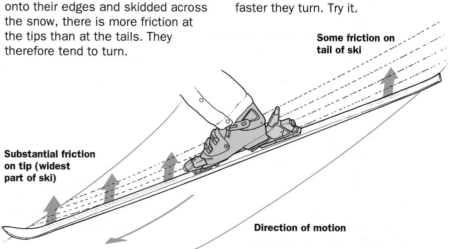

Some friction on tail of ski

Substantial friction on tip (widest part of ski)

Direction of motion

1 Start in a shallow traverse in the standard traverse stance.

2 Push out both skis into a gliding snowplough.

3 Sink slightly and steer your skis into the fall line, edging your outside ski strongly and allowing the pressure to shift off your inside ski.

4 Bring your inside ski parallel to your outside ski.

5 Continue the turn in a controlled, parallel skid. Keep the pressure firmly on your outside ski.

6 Rise back up into the standard traverse position ready for the next turn

THE BASIC SWING STOP

Until now, one of your most pressing concerns has probably been how to stop. The basic swing stop is quick and effective. Starting with a basic swing turn away from the fall line, bring your skis rapidly across your direction of travel and skid to a halt using your uphill edges.

The easiest way to learn the basic swing stop is to try it first from a shallow traverse. Once you have mastered this, set off in steeper and steeper traverses, until you can stop from the fall line.

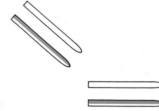

TIPS

■ Before attempting the basic swing stop, you should be comfortable with sideslipping and the basic swing turn.
■ Your skis must be brought across the direction of travel rapidly, or you will end up turning, not stopping.
■ Make sure that you stay on your uphill edges throughout. Catching a downhill edge almost always results in a fall.
■ As you come to rest, stand up and allow your body to catch up with your skis to avoid falling over towards the hill.
■ Practise stopping to both right and left. Most skiers have one stronger side that they naturally favour; the problem is, you may not always have the luxury of choice.
■ Never stop above a group of people: you may misjudge your speed or hit a patch of ice, and the resulting accident will be totally your fault. In any case, the humour of showering everyone with snow is unoriginal.

1 Begin a basic swing turn uphill (away from the fall line).

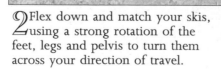

2 Flex down and match your skis, using a strong rotation of the feet, legs and pelvis to turn them across your direction of travel.

3 Remain flexed as you skid to a stop, balancing against the braking resistance of your uphill edges.

'Nothing to Fear but Fear Itself'

Many beginners spend their first few days on skis in a paroxysm of fear; even experienced skiers live through the occasional moment of terror.

A realistic fear of injury is useful: it is your body's protective mechanism at work. But more often, fear results simply from unfamiliar surroundings or from the feeling of sliding. This is unproductive. The way to learn is to concentrate on the sensations of your skiing, and fear blocks your ability to do this.

■ Avoid slopes that are well beyond your capability.

■ Stop before you become excessively tired.

■ Talk yourself down slopes that you know you can ski.

■ Be realistic about the consequences of a fall.

■ Always take the time to look around and enjoy your surroundings.

If you continue to be tense and nervous, there are a number of learning methods that may be of use. These use techniques to focus your attention on kinesthetic sensations (the sensations arising from forces in your body), while blocking out worries and self-advice. The best known of these methods is called Inner Skiing, (after the book by Timothy Gallwey and Bob Kriegel, Bantam Books).

A longer way to fall.

The Uphill Stem Turn

SPEEDING UP YOUR EDGE CHANGES

The uphill stem is an advanced variant of the basic swing that speeds up the initiation of the turn. This reduces the time spent in the fall line, and hence the acceleration you experience on steeper slopes. It is also less tiring, as it involves a less pronounced snowplough. In North America, it is known as a pointing christie.

Instead of performing the initial snowplough with both skis, you push only the uphill ski into a narrow half-snowplough, called a stem. This points your uphill ski into the turn. Shifting pressure onto your outside ski allows you to match your inside ski, and the turn can be completed very quickly with a parallel skid.

Since the uphill stem incorporates a distinct initiation (when the pressure is removed from the downhill ski), introducing a pole plant at this point can help with timing and balance (see pages 106-107).

The uphill stem turn can be performed at almost any speed. It will help you to develop many of the technical ingredients of advanced skiing: most importantly, quick edge changes and more subtle steering of the feet and legs. It can take your skiing a very long way; indeed, the step turn used by Alpine racers (see page 152) is a natural development of the uphill stem.

TIPS

■ The timing of the uphill stem is like taking a sideways step: first you push your uphill ski out, then you bring your downhill ski parallel. As you build experience, eliminate the time between the steps, reducing the effort required to perform the turn.
■ The pole plant is intended to help your stability as you transfer your weight from one ski to the other.
■ If the snow surface allows it, simply slide your outside ski into the stem, otherwise lift the tail clear of the snow and pivot the ski around the tip.

EXERCISE

■ Eliminate the traverse between turns. As you finish each turn, push the new uphill ski straight out to start the next. Get into a rhythm: stem and plant, match and sink; stem and plant, match and sink.

IMAGE AND SELF-IMAGE

Many skiers are handicapped because they worry about how they look to other people. Do I look stupid? Do I look out of control? Is the lift queue impressed?

It is never worth worrying about how you look. Ski for yourself: if it feels relaxed, powerful and precise, then it is good skiing. Concentrate on these sensations. What type of skiing generates them? What prevents you from feeling them? If you can answer these questions, your skiing will rapidly improve.

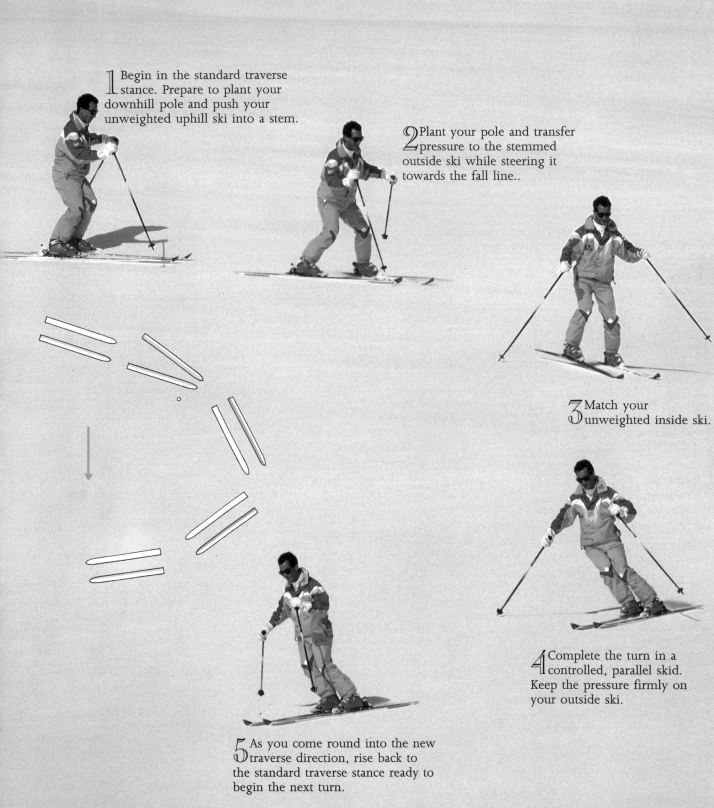

1 Begin in the standard traverse stance. Prepare to plant your downhill pole and push your unweighted uphill ski into a stem.

2 Plant your pole and transfer pressure to the stemmed outside ski while steering it towards the fall line..

3 Match your unweighted inside ski.

4 Complete the turn in a controlled, parallel skid. Keep the pressure firmly on your outside ski.

5 As you come round into the new traverse direction, rise back to the standard traverse stance ready to begin the next turn.

PLANTING YOUR POLES

The pole is the most misunderstood and misused piece of ski equipment. Many skiers carry their poles without any real understanding of their use. Others use their poles in such a way that they hinder rather than help effective turning.

THE POLE PLANT

The pole plant serves three purposes in a turn:
■ Ensuring correct positioning of your body by moving your weight forwards and down the fall line.
■ Providing stability by giving you an extra point of support as you transfer pressure from one ski to the other, and from one edge to the other.
■ Acting as a trigger to time the beginning of your turn.

CARRYING YOUR POLES

Your hands must be in front of you at all times. If you can't see them in your peripheral vision, they are either too low, or behind you. Imagine you are holding the steering wheel of a bus, with your arms in front of you and slightly bent, and your poles will be in the right place. At first you may feel a little unnatural in the 'steering wheel' position. Persevere, and quite soon it will be second nature.

WHERE TO PLANT YOUR POLE

To be effective, your pole plant must be ahead of you, but far enough from your skis so you don't ski over the basket. The optimal position will vary with the type of turn, speed of skiing and steepness of the slope. You should plant somewhere on an arc which leads from your ski tips to a point about two feet to the side of your boots. The faster you are skiing, the further forward you should aim to plant your pole.

Very steep skiing

Moguls, short radius turns

Fast, long radius turns

Always keep your hands in front of you, ready to plant your poles.

Classic faults include holding your poles behind your body where they are totally useless for any manoeuvre.

1 Hold your arms in the 'steering wheel' position, then anticipate the coming pole plant.

2 Use a movement from the wrist to bring the basket into contact with the snow. Tense your arm momentarily to take the impact, but keep any movement of the arm to a minimum.

HOW TO PLANT YOUR POLE

The firmness with which you should plant the pole depends on your speed and the type of turn: for fast turns on flat terrain the poles need hardly touch the snow, whereas for mogul skiing you will require a very positive, even aggressive, pole plant.

More important than the force used is the movement with which you plant the pole. This begins with an anticipation phase, in which the downhill pole is angled forwards to point at the spot where it will be planted. The pole is planted with a movement from the wrist that brings the basket into contact with the snow; it is released similarly by a movement from the wrist as you pass. There should be very little involvement from the elbow and none at all from the shoulder.

3 Keep your arm forward so the planted pole pivots about its basket as you ski past it.

WHEN TO PLANT YOUR POLE

The pole plant should be timed to provide stability as you begin your turn. This means that the basket must always hit the snow just prior to your switching pressure to the outside ski.

EXERCISE

■ Walking your poles. Choose a very shallow slope and ski straight down the fall line. Starting with both arms in the neutral position, walk your poles down the slope, planting them one after the other. Keep your arms forward throughout and get a feel for using only your wrists.

4 Release the pole by continuing the movement from the wrist. You are back in the neutral, 'steering wheel' position.

YOUR FIRST MOGULS

NEGOTIATING THE BUMPS USING UPHILL STEM TURNS

Any slope that is used by a large number of skiers develops moguls, or bumps (the two terms are synonymous). The process starts when, by chance, a few skiers turn in the same place. They carve a gentle dip and create a tiny mound. Successive skiers find it easier to turn in the same place, and each scrapes out the dip a little more and pushes up the mound a little further. Soon the snow is sculpted into a series of pronounced bumps.

The uphill stem turn allows you to make your first sorties into this landscape. The key lies in timing your turn so that you take advantage of the terrain. Make your first attempts on isolated bumps on shallow slopes, before venturing into more difficult mogul fields. The uphill stem is a versatile turn and can be used in quite extreme bumps.

TIPS

■ Time your turn for the crest of the mogul. Stem too early and you will have to work hard to steer your skis; stem too late and you will be thrown off balance by passing over the crest of the mogul.
■ Don't leave your pole planted for too long: this will pull your arm behind you and throw you off balance.
■ Try to turn on every mogul. Once you miss one, your rhythm is ruined.

THE MOGUL EMPIRE

No two mogul fields are the same. The distance between the bumps depends on the steepness of the slope and the proficiency of the skiers. Their size depends on the snow conditions and the density of skier traffic.

Similarly, no two bumps are identical. All are, however, formed in the same way: the repeated passage of skiers scrapes snow from the trough and pushes it up onto the front of the mogul.

Almost all bumps share the same characteristics.

Sharp crest, pointing down the fall line

Top, covered in soft snow

Soft front (uphill)

Hard, scraped downhill flanks

Steep back (downhill)

Smooth trough, leading to front of next bump

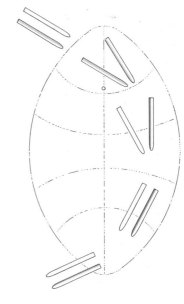

1 Begin in the standard traverse stance. Choose your mogul and approach the uphill face. Bring your pole forwards to anticipate the pole plant.

2 As you pass over the mogul, push your unweighted uphill ski into a stem and plant your pole.

3 Transfer pressure onto the stemmed ski, steering it towards the fall line. Release the pole as you pass it.

4 Match your inside ski. Flex down and complete the turn in a controlled, parallel skid down the far side of the mogul.

5 As you finish your turn, rise back up into the standard traverse stance and plot your route to the next turn.

ADVANCED SCHUSS POSITIONS

MOVING AT SPEED

As you start to experiment with higher speeds, you are ready to try a more advanced schuss position. The tuck, or egg, offers the optimum aerodynamic position, but still allows the use of the edges to steer. It is fun and fast but quite tiring for the thighs, back and neck. In addition, shock absorption is limited, and unexpected bumps and hollows can provide unpleasant surprises for the inexperienced.

SPEED AND SAFETY

Travelling effortlessly at high speed is one of the great attractions of skiing. But speed brings with it an element of danger. Always be aware of this.
■ Keep your speed down on crowded slopes.
■ Keep your speed down in bad visibility.
■ Keep your speed down if you are tired.
■ Keep your speed down around blind corners or over drop-offs.
■ Give other skiers a wide berth: even if you don't hit them, you may scare them.
■ Never ski beyond the limits of your equipment. Short skis, loose bindings and high speeds are a recipe for disaster.

Use a neat, compact tuck to achieve a high-speed schuss.

Head up, eyes forwards

Arms pushed forwards

Elbows in front of knees (nothing is less cool than tucking with your elbows firmly pressed into your stomach)

Knees bent at right angles and brought up under the chest

Though not as fast as the tuck, the pike position is much less strenuous. It is especially useful for long, shallow schusses.

SKATING

Skating offers a quick way to cross a flat area or climb a gentle rise. It is much faster than walking, though more tiring. Skating on skis is just like ice skating. If you are comfortable with herringbone climbing, you will find it easy: it is the same movement, with the introduction of a glide at the end of each step.

TIPS

- Don't stay too long on one ski. Maintain your momentum.
- Add power by bringing the lifted leg in before thrusting out for each step.
- If you find skating impossible, go back and revise your herringbone climbing (see page 98).

EXERCISE

- Can you skate without using your poles? This ensures that you are transferring your weight correctly and using the power of your legs.

1 Lift one ski and plant both poles. Push on your poles and project the lifted ski diagonally outwards and forwards.

2 Transfer your weight onto the new ski and lift the other, ready for the next step.

11 · PISTE CRAFT

As you begin to roam more widely, and especially as you begin to ski
without an instructor, you become responsible for ensuring your
own enjoyable and safe skiing. It's up to you to find the combination
of technical challenge, relaxation and mountain experience
that suits you best.

In order to find your way around your resort, always ski with a piste map. These are available free of charge at the local tourist office, or at lift ticket booths.

Pistes are marked according to a colour-coded system, which varies slightly between Europe and North America (see right). While these markings are intended to help you to select suitable slopes, don't take them for granted. In poor conditions a blue run can seem more like a red one. Also, a red run in a challenging resort like Chamonix might be as difficult as a black run at a more gentle resort such as Megève.

The markers down the side of the piste are usually in the appropriate colour. They bear the name or number of the piste, so you can locate it on your piste map, and the poles should also be numbered.

In case of an accident, note the number of the nearest pole, so you can identify the scene accurately to the rescue services.

On the slopes, the following markings are fairly universal and should never be ignored:
- Black and yellow striped poles: rocks or other obstacles.

TYPE OF RUN		
	Europe	**North America**
Very easy (beginner)	▬ Green	● Green circle
Easy (early intermediate)	▬ Blue	▪ Blue square
Medium (advanced intermediate)	▬ Red	◆ Black diamond
Difficult (advanced)	▬ Black	◆◆ Double black diamond
Off piste/unpatrolled route	••• Dotted	–

NOTE: *These may vary slightly between resorts*

- Black and yellow chequered or plain black flags: avalanche danger.
- Ropes: severe dangers, such as cliffs or crevasses; closed runs.
- Crossed skis: injured skier on the slope.

Ski patrollers, or *pisteurs*, take care of piste maintenance. This includes grooming runs with piste machines (often called ratracs), sign-posting, marking rocks and crevasses, and controlling avalanches with explosives. They are responsible for your overall safety and for bringing injured skiers down if necessary. They are not responsible if you go off piste or ignore their warnings.

MEET THE MOUNTAINS

If you are having difficulty finding your way around your ski area, help should be at hand. In North America, most resorts supply hosts and hostesses, whose ideal-sounding job is to cruise around the slopes, encouraging you to have a nice day. In Europe, the Ski Club of Great Britain (SCGB) has representatives in most large resorts who provide free guiding for members. Many tour operators also offer a free service for their clients; failing this, why not get a group together and hire a guide?

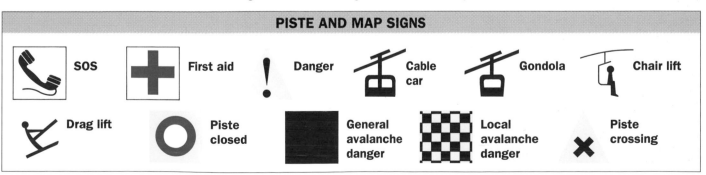

PISTE AND MAP SIGNS

SOS — First aid — ! Danger — Cable car — Gondola — Chair lift

Drag lift — Piste closed — General avalanche danger — Local avalanche danger — Piste crossing

Glacier skiing, good snow but can be cold and windy. Usually easy slopes. Open in summer.

Boundary between two resorts: check when the lift closes and make sure you leave enough time to get back to your valley. Otherwise, you could be in for an expensive taxi ride.

Pistes through the trees: good in a white-out but may be icy. If narrow, avoid last thing in the afternoon.

Large concentration of blue and green runs: good area for beginners and intermediates. Crowded last run down.

Beginners' slopes. Fairly flat and close to the village.

Very high skiing. Good view, but could be very cold. Too high to try on your first day.

South-facing slopes: warm, but may be slushy.

Off-piste itineraries: you're on your own here.

Relatively low pistes: warmer temperatures may mean stones and slush, or even insufficient snow cover.

STADES OLYMPIQUES

TIGNES 2100

CHOOSING YOUR LINE

When descending any slope, the line you choose can have a strong influence on the quality of your skiing. By looking ahead and planning your route, you can pick out the best terrain to exercise your skiing skills.

Pick your route carefully.

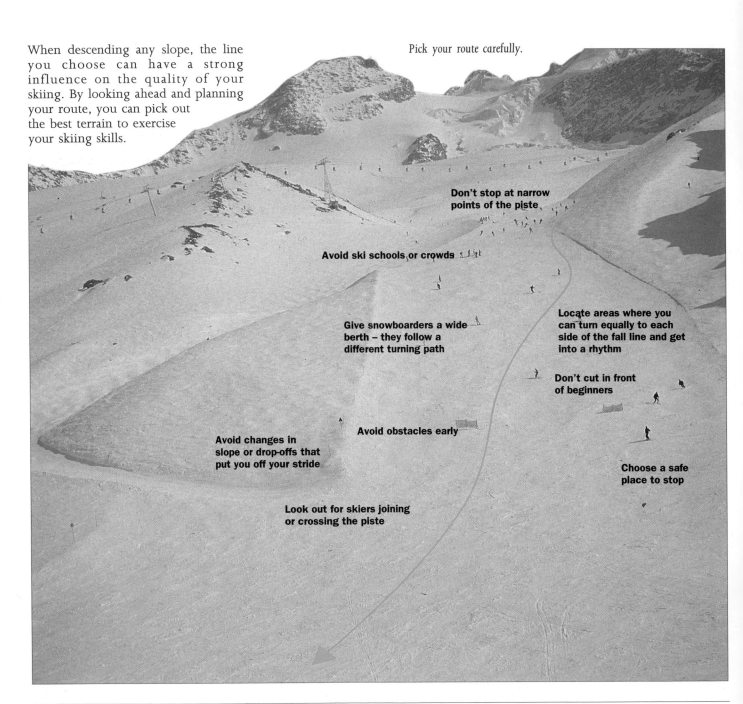

Don't stop at narrow points of the piste

Avoid ski schools or crowds

Give snowboarders a wide berth – they follow a different turning path

Locate areas where you can turn equally to each side of the fall line and get into a rhythm

Don't cut in front of beginners

Avoid obstacles early

Avoid changes in slope or drop-offs that put you off your stride

Choose a safe place to stop

Look out for skiers joining or crossing the piste

PISTE ETIQUETTE

THE FIS CODE OF CONDUCT

The International Ski Federation (FIS) has developed a set of rules governing the conduct of skiers.

1 Respect for others. A skier must behave in such a way that he does not endanger or prejudice others. (Note that potentially dangerous skiers are assumed to be male throughout!)

2 Control of speed and skiing. A skier must ski in control. He must adapt his speed and manner of skiing to his personal ability and to the prevailing conditions of terrain, snow and weather as well as to the density of traffic.

3 Choice of route. A skier coming from behind must choose his route in such a way that he does not endanger skiers ahead. (In other words, the skier in front/below always has priority.)

4 Overtaking. A skier may overtake another skier above or below and to the right or the left, provided that he leaves enough space for the overtaken skier to make any voluntary or involuntary movement.

5 Entering and starting. A skier entering a marked run or starting again after stopping must look up and down the run to make sure that he can do so without endangering himself or others.

6 Stopping on the piste. Unless absolutely necessary, a skier must avoid stopping on the piste in narrow places or where visibility is restricted. After a fall in such a place, a skier must move clear of the piste as soon as possible.

7 Climbing and descending on foot. Whether climbing or descending on foot, the skier must keep to the side of the piste.

8 Respect for signs and markings. A skier must respect all signs and markings at all times.

9 Assistance. At accidents every skier is duty-bound to assist.

10 Identification. Every skier and witness, whether a responsible party or not, must exchange names and addresses following an accident.

FEAR OF COLLISIONS

Rule three of the FIS code points out that the skier below/ahead has priority. Although this usually means in practice that the slower skier has right of way, it's not worth pushing your luck: collisions are amongst the nastiest of accidents.
- Don't stop round blind corners.
- Don't stop near icy patches.
- Clear difficult stretches of the piste as quickly as possible.
- Try to be aware of the movements of other skiers.

DAYLIGHT ROBBERY

Even rented or old skis are worth protecting, if only to avoid the inconvenience of being stranded without them.

Particularly vulnerable areas are restaurants at the summit station of a cable car or in the village. Keep your skis within sight, or swap one with a friend, leaving the unmatched pairs in different places. Never leave your skis unattended for extended periods or overnight.

Locks are available, though not customary in Europe. Many resorts have lockable racks or lockers at the base of the lifts so you don't have to carry your skis to and from the slopes every day.

WEATHER CONDITIONS

LEARNING TO RESPECT THE MOUNTAIN ENVIRONMENT

Up in the mountains the weather is not just a topic of conversation. On its vagaries depend your comfort, enjoyment and, most importantly, your safety.

Conditions can change rapidly, and are difficult to predict for those who are not familiar with the area. Check the weather forecast each day before setting out, so you know what to expect and how to dress. It is usually posted outside the local tourist bureau, and read out on local radio several times each morning.

If in doubt about what to wear, put on an extra layer and take a backpack, so you can strip off if you become too hot. It is better to be too warm than too cold.

TIPS

- Clear nights are invariably followed by cold mornings.
- Moderate wind in the resort means high winds at altitude.
- Ultraviolet light can penetrate thin cloud cover, so always protect your skin and eyes.
- When it is snowing, visibility above the tree line will be minimal.

THE WHITE WAY UP

Skiing in a white-out – snow, mist or fog – can be an unnerving experience. Without a horizon, you lose orientation, confusing up and down. Moguls become invisible, speed impossible to judge.

Many skiers give up at this point, retreating to the café to await better weather, but skiing in these conditions can be fun, as long as you take the necessary precautions:

- Stay below the tree line (where there is some contrast) or stick to slopes you know well.
- Ski in a group and always remain in visual contact with the skier in front.
- Stop frequently and count the members of the group to avoid losing anyone.
- Ski from one piste marker to the next.
- Adopt a wide stance, pressure on both skis, ready to react quickly to the terrain.
- Concentrate on the feelings in your feet: they are in closest contact with the snow.

Skiing in a white-out

The State of the Slopes

SNOW CONDITIONS ON PISTE

Although all self-respecting snow-flakes share the same six-pointed geometry, it is said that no two are ever identical. A snowflake is formed in the clouds when supercooled water vapour condenses and freezes, usually onto a microscopic foreign body, such as a particle of dust. More vapour condenses onto the flake until it begins to fall because of its weight. The ultimate size of the flake depends on the surrounding humidity and temperature – the colder the temperature, the smaller the flake.

Once a snowflake has landed, it begins to transform. Slowly, its sharp edges become rounded and it begins to merge with neighbouring flakes; the snow's surface texture changes. Snow conditions build up over a period of months, and can be hard to grasp in a week's holiday. Conditions alter with time of year and of day, and different pistes are better in different seasons. In general, most north-facing slopes will have good, dry snow, but will tend to be cold. South-facing slopes are a good bet in mid-winter, but in spring they tend to be icy early in the morning and slushy in the afternoon. East- and west-facing slopes present a combination of these conditions.

Skiing on piste, there are a number of different types of snow that you will encounter (for off-piste conditions, see pages 180-181).

PACKED POWDER

This is what good piste skiing is all about. Over the days after a good, dry snowfall, the powder is packed either by skier traffic or by a ratrac. The result is a perfect surface: firm enough to bear your edges with precision, yet yielding and painless to fall on.

SLUSH

At the end of every season, or during any warm spell, the snow turns to slush. Individual crystals of snow have fused with their neighbours to form little balls of ice, floating in a wet, watery paste.

Skiing becomes hard work and the risk of injury is increased. But you can still have fun: let your skis run and use a little extra speed to make them plane over the slush.

ARTIFICIAL SNOW

To protect their business from the vagaries of the weather, resorts are increasingly installing snow cannons (although even these require adequate water and low temperatures). The snow produced is much more dense than natural snow, making it less forgiving and more likely to become icy. Despite these shortcomings, and the strong environmental arguments against it, artificial snow looks like it is here to stay.

ICE

The snow condition most dreaded by the majority of skiers is ice (see page 120). South-facing slopes, which have been warmed by the previous afternoon's sun, will frequently be icy in the morning and refreeze again once the sun leaves them in the afternoon. Slopes that are exposed to high winds will also be among the first to become icy, as will those that carry the greatest amount of skier traffic.

Snowflakes, as seen using false colour scanning electron micrograph.

Skiing on Ice

THE SKIER'S NIGHTMARE

Skiing on ice need not be something to dread, though few would claim to enjoy it. Your best plan is to avoid ice altogether. Even if this is impossible, there are usually ways of skirting the worst. The edges of a piste tend to have better snow than the middle. Similarly, the outside edge of a path is frequently free from ice even when the uphill edge is bullet-proof. You may even be able to drop over the edge and traverse in a deep layer of snow that has been pushed off the path.

If you do find yourself on a patch of ice, you will begin to accelerate. Most skiers' reaction is to try to brake. However, almost all patches of ice end in a pile of snow, pushed up by other skiers. Let your skis run straight across the ice and put in your next turn only when you reach the sanctuary of this pile of snow.

Occasionally, conditions may be so bad that you really are skiing continuously on ice, and there will be no way to avoid turning. It is still possible to retain control of your skis: when you next switch on the television and see the racers performing their precise, flowing turns, bear in mind that the surface they are on is probably as hard as boiler-plate.

Try the following techniques:
■ Modify your stance: keeping your skis further apart not only enhances your balance, but also allows your inside ski to act as insurance in case your outside ski slips away.
■ Ensure your weight is distributed evenly between your skis and use the entire length of your edges by keeping your weight in the middle.

Keeping to the outside edge of a path can often help you to avoid ice.

■ Be very subtle in your skiing: any sharp movements will result in your edges breaking their tenuous grip on the ice.
■ Don't over-steer your skis: they steer very easily, and can rapidly end up across your direction of travel; once this happens, you will have little option but to slip sideways until your edges grip.
■ Make sure that your edges are super-sharp (for information on ski maintenance, see page 43).

Try to avoid turning on ice patches. If this is impossible, adopt a wide stance.

12 · PARALLEL TURNS

The aim of most intermediate skiers is to perform parallel turns on any slope and in any conditions. Parallel turns are the most elegant and efficient way to ski. By letting gravity and your skis do the work, you exert only such effort as is required to steer and brake. You remain relaxed and fluid while performing powerful, precise turns.

With a bit of application and a varying amount of practice, anyone can ski parallel. There is nothing wrong with continuing to use your basic swing and uphill stem turns on more difficult terrain, while practising parallel turns on shallower slopes.

The Basic Parallel Turn

ELIMINATING THE SNOWPLOUGH

1 Start in the standard
traverse stance.

The basic parallel is an easy introduction to parallel skiing, and well suited to most slopes. The turn is initiated by switching the pressure from your downhill ski to what will become the outside ski of the turn. A pole plant with the downhill pole provides you with stability as you begin to steer your skis into the fall line. The turn is completed just like a basic swing or uphill stem, by applying your edges and steering the skidding skis with your feet and legs. Your shoulders face down the fall line throughout.

TIPS

■ Don't be obsessed with keeping your skis parallel. What is important is not the angle of the skis to each other but the simultaneous timing of the edge change. Concentrate on timing the steering and edging.
■ Practise pressuring your outside ski as early as possible, even before you have begun your turn. Once the pressure is on the inside edge of this ski, you will find steering it into the fall line, and beginning the turn, easy.
■ Steer your skis into the fall line using only your legs and feet. Don't use your upper body. Throwing your shoulders round will only make you over-rotate your turns.
■ Keep your hands in front of you at all times, always within your field of vision (for planting your poles, see page 123).
■ Many skiers complain that they find it difficult to eradicate the final vestiges of stem turns from their skiing. This is mainly a matter of practice on shallow slopes; there is no point in trying an unfamiliar technique on a steep slope.
■ Try to hit a rhythm when you link your basic parallels. This will result in a tremendous feeling of flowing down the slope.

COLD SNAPS

Although photographs of your skiing holiday make great souvenirs, many skiers are put off by the thought of carrying a camera. Small, fully automatic cameras are compact enough to fit into a pocket and can take very good photos. If you do use an SLR camera, the ideal lens is probably a 35-105mm (or similar) zoom, which will enable you to take both landscape and action shots.

It is important to look after your films - they mustn't get wet, nor too cold as they become brittle and may break on loading. In general there is plenty of light, so a standard film speed (such as 100 ASA for prints, 64 ASA for slides) will provide the best sharpness. For action shots, pre-focus on the spot where the skier will be. To capture the angle of a steep slope, shoot from the side or above, and try to include the horizon or some trees.

But how can you make the skies really blue and bring out the brightness of the snow? Shooting in the late afternoon takes advantage of enhanced shadows and contrast. The extreme brightness of the background, however, can fool the metering system of your camera and leave you with underexposed photos. If the camera has an adjustable aperture setting, take a light reading of the snow and then open the aperture one and a half stops. Alternatively, use the backlighting adjustment which even many basic models now offer.

With a simpler camera, you can achieve the same effect by setting a false film speed: for instance, use a 100 ASA film but set the camera for 50 ASA. This will slow down the shutter, exposing the subjects of your photos correctly and bringing out the brightness of the snow.

2 Anticipate the pole plant with the downhill arm.

3 Plant the downhill pole and switch the pressure from your downhill to your uphill ski.

4 Steer your skis towards the fall line.

5 Apply your edges and complete the turn in a controlled, parallel skid.

6 As you finish the turn, look ahead to select a spot for your next turn.

The Fan Method

AN EASY WAY TO LEARN THE BASIC PARALLEL

The fan method provides a simple way of learning the basic parallel turn. It breaks the turn down into its constituent parts, which are then easily learnt in reverse order.

First you turn up the hill from a shallow traverse (A). This is called an uphill christie or swing to the hill, and builds on your sideslipping skills. You then perform swings to the hill from steeper and steeper traverses, until you are turning out of the fall line (B). Finally you turn right through the fall line (C). The name fan method comes from the tracks left in the snow.

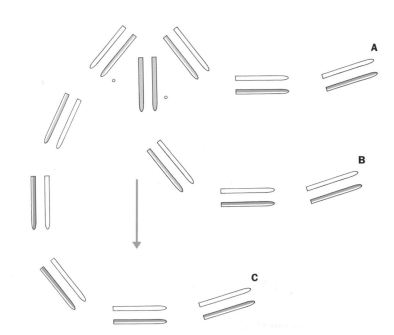

Turn uphill from a shallow traverse and swing to the hill(A), then increase the angle of the traverse until you are turning out from the fall line (B) and finally from a shallow traverse facing the other way turning through the fall line (C).

1 Start off in the basic traverse stance.

A SWING TO THE HILL

Start in a gentle traverse, flex down slightly to release your edge and steer the tips of your skis uphill in a parallel swing to the hill. Since the pressure remains on the same ski throughout, this should be straightforward. Gradually increase the angle of traverse. Soon you will be performing your swing to the hill directly from the fall line.

2 Keeping the pressure on your downhill ski, flex slightly and steer the tips of your skis uphill. Allow your skis to break into a controlled, parallel skid.

3 Continue your swing to the hill, controlling it until you stop.

1 Set out in the fall line in the basic stance. Bring your pole forwards to anticipate the plant.

B INTRODUCE A POLE PLANT

Once you feel comfortable with your swings to the hill to left and right from the fall line, it is time to introduce a pole plant.

BRAKING IN A TRAVERSE

The swing to the hill is useful to control speed in a traverse. Use it to change from a pure traverse into a forward sideslip. Once you have lost sufficient speed, steer your tips back into the direction of travel. This is less tiring than a snow-plough, and allows greater control.

2 Plant the pole, move the pressure to your outside ski, beginning to steer your skis out of the fall line.

3 Continue the turn just like a swing to the hill in a controlled parallel skid.

4 Complete the turn by bringing yourself to a stop.

C TURN THROUGH THE FALL LINE

All you need to do now is to perform the same turn through the fall line. Set out in a steep traverse, plant your pole, weight the new outside ski and steer into the fall line. Then use the swing to the hill to come out of the fall line and stop. You have just performed a complete basic parallel turn!

Keep practising until you can perform basic parallels to left and right from shallow traverses.

TIPS

■ If you have a weaker side, spend more time practising in that direction.
■ If you find it hard to control your swing to the hill, go back and practise diagonal sideslipping (see page 94).

ANGULATION

BALANCING AGAINST CENTRIFUGAL FORCE

As you perform any turn, your skis have to be displaced to the outside of the turn so that you can balance against the centrifugal force. The way in which you achieve this is called angulation. It's similar to riding a bicycle when you lean inwards to balance against the centrifugal force of a turn.

You have been using angulation since your first basic swing turns (see page 100), probably without thinking about it. Initially, you didn't need very much angulation since, at low speeds, you didn't experience much in the way of lateral force, and your weight was always fairly squarely over your skis for balance. As your skiing starts to become more dynamic, you must use more angulation.

Knee angulation is quick and easy to control. Use it for shorter radius turns.

Hip angulation is much more powerful, but takes longer to get from one turn into the next. You will use it increasingly for longer radius turns (see chapter 14, page 146).

Whole body angulation (or banking) requires very little effort, though you must have great sensitivity to steer your skis. You also have to be sure that your edges will hold!

Outside foot　　　　　　**Inside foot**

With your feet locked together, the extent to which you can set your skis onto their edges is limited, because as you roll your knees, you cannot put enough pressure on your outside foot.

HOW MANY FEET APART?

Many people believe that good parallel skiing means keeping your feet locked together at all times. Frequently beginners or poor intermediates will select a skier who can negotiate the nursery slopes with skis chattering against each other as their model of an advanced skier.

They couldn't be more wrong. To start with, a wider stance improves your balance: chairs topple over, tables don't. But perhaps even more importantly, good edge control requires two things: the ability to roll the skis easily and quickly onto their edges, and the ability to put pressure on a carefully targeted part of the skis' edges. Skiing

with your feet too close together impedes both of these actions.

Try the following experiment: with your feet locked together, flex down and try rolling your knees to the side to simulate setting your skis on edge. Then try the same move with your feet 15-20cm (6-8 in) apart (see right).

In short, you should not worry about how wide apart your skis are. Concentrate instead on the fundamentals of your parallel turns. If you get these right, your inside ski will be flat and unweighted as you perform your turn. It should float towards your outside ski under the influence of centrifugal force, with very little exertion on your part, and without interfering with your body's natural movements.

Outside foot　　　　　　**Inside foot**

On the other hand, if you start with your feet 15-20cm (6-8 in) apart, it is easy to roll onto your edges and place the pressure firmly where it should be: on the inside edge of your outside foot.

UNWEIGHTING

MANIPULATING THE FORCE ON YOUR SKIS

Throughout the basic parallel turn your body weight acts through your skis. You shift the pressure from one ski to the other as you roll onto your new edges, but your weight continues to push them firmly into the snow. This is a smooth and controlled way to make your turns, but it is not the only technique used.

Momentarily lightening the pressure on your skis can both speed up the initiation of your turns and reduce the effort required, allowing your skis to pivot easily, irrespective of the slope and nature of the surface. This is called unweighting. It is a useful weapon in your skiing armoury, and one you should master.

A word of warning though: each moment your skis are unweighted is a moment when their edges cannot be used to control your speed or direction. Although unweighting can make life easy, it can also be a barrier to improvement and to developing more advanced, carved turns.

There are four different types of unweighting, each appropriate to different types of turn and terrain.

UP-UNWEIGHTING

This is the most common method, and the first one to learn. In order to up-unweight, extend upwards from a flexed position. It is like performing a little jump, though your feet don't actually have to leave the ground, just become light for an instant. Try up-unweighting to initiate easy, lazy turns on smooth slopes.

Unweighted

From the basic stance...   ...flex down smoothly...   ...then extend upwards to take your weight off your feet.

TERRAIN UNWEIGHTING

The next important type is terrain unweighting. Instead of fully absorbing a ridge or mogul, stiffen slightly and allow it to project your weight up off your feet. It should feel like driving over a speed bump too fast in a car. Terrain unweighting is the easiest way of beginning a turn on slopes that are not quite smooth.

Unweighted

Approaching a bump... *...instead of absorbing, stiffen...* *...and allow it to project the pressure off your feet.*

REBOUND UNWEIGHTING

When skidding down a slope, suddenly set a powerful edge. Your skis brake sharply but your body continues to move; your weight is thrown up off your skis. It's a bit like slamming on the front brake of a bicycle, translating your forward motion into upward motion! Rebound unweighting is very useful in shortening the radius of your turns on steep slopes or in moguls.

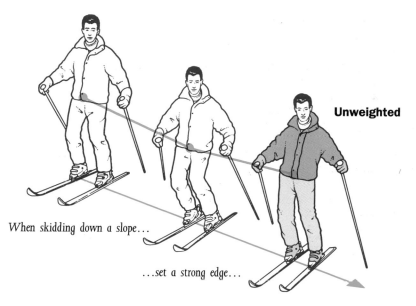

Unweighted

When skidding down a slope...

...set a strong edge...

...and your weight will be thrown up off your skis.

DOWN-UNWEIGHTING

This consists of standing tall and then suddenly dropping your centre of mass by flexing at the knees and hips. The feeling is similar to when a lift begins to descend: as your centre of mass drops, the pressure on your feet is reduced momentarily. Down-unweighting is usually a very subtle movement, which can be useful when you want to ski very smoothly, such as on ice or in long-radius turns.

Unweighted

From a tall position... *...suddenly allow your centre of mass to drop.*

THE HOCKEY STOP

PUTTING THE BRAKES ON

1 Start by skiing down the fall line in the basic stance.

The hockey stop is very similar to the basic swing stop (see page 102), the only difference being that your skis remain parallel throughout.

The easiest way to learn it is by practising first from a traverse. As your familiarity increases, try it from steeper and steeper traverses until you can do it from the fall line. Use strong up-unweighting and swivel your skis right across your direction of travel; then apply your edges to bring yourself to a sharp halt.

2 Flex down in preparation for up-unweighting your skis.

3 Up-unweight strongly. Keeping your upper body facing down the fall line, turn your skis across the direction of travel using a strong rotation of the feet, legs and pelvis.

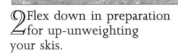

As you spend more time on snow you may start looking for a new challenge. Tricks can be fun and can also improve your normal skiing, as they focus your attention where it should be: on your skis, edges and on the sensations in your feet.

Can you perform a turn on your inside ski only? How about the Charleston (linked inside ski turns to left and right)? A 360-degree spin?

If you enjoy trying these tricks, ski ballet may be for you (see page 192). There are many clubs where you can meet other interested skiers and be coached. In Britain, many dry slopes have ballet clubs.

Julia Snell, Britain's top ballet skier, showing the form which made her a World Cup winner.

4 Remain flexed as you skid to a stop, balancing against the braking resistance. As you come to rest, stand up and allow your body to catch up with your skis to avoid falling towards the hill.

THE TERRAIN PARALLEL

SKIING PARALLEL IN THE MOGULS

As your parallel skiing becomes more confident you can tackle more challenging terrain, such as moguls. The secret lies in using terrain unweighting (see page 129) to take advantage of any little hump or ridge to begin your turns.

Practise on a gentle slope with very few bumps or moguls. Plan your path in advance, looking well ahead. Choose an appropriate bump, and plant your pole on the very top to help you to balance as your skis pass over the crest. As your skis become unweighted, begin the turn by rolling your skis onto their new edges and steering them into the fall line. Complete the turn by skidding down the far side of the bump.

Once you feel comfortable using the occasional bump to help you to unweight, you are ready to venture into an easy mogul field using your terrain parallels.

TIPS

■ Look well ahead and anticipate each turn. Concentrate on feeling the forces on your feet so that you are ready for the instant of weightlessness.
■ Time your steering and edge change to coincide with your boots' passing over the crest of the bump. Start your turn too early and you will have to work hard to steer your skis into the fall line; start your turn too late and you will be thrown off balance as you pass over the crest of the mogul.

■ Finish each turn by skidding down the far side of the bump. When you have spent more time in moguls, you will be able to master more advanced techniques (see chapter 15, page 159).

ARE YOU A DOOR OPENER?

Many common faults that arise in advanced skiing can be directly traced to technical weaknesses in skiing on the flat. By far the most common example of this is leaving the poles planted in the snow for too long during each turn. This causes the inside arm to get pulled far behind you, rotating out from the shoulder in an action reminiscent of opening a door outwards, away from the body.

At worst, 'opening doors' can cause a catastrophic loss of balance. At best, it will make you over-rotate the turn, leaving you unable to begin your next turn where you want.

Avoid leaving your pole planted for too long.

1 Start in a standard traverse stance on a slope with a few well separated moguls. Look ahead to select a mogul on which to turn.

2 Plant your pole on the crest of the chosen mogul. Tense your legs slightly as your skis begin to ride up the mogul, allowing your weight to be projected up off your skis (terrain unweighting).

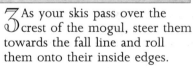

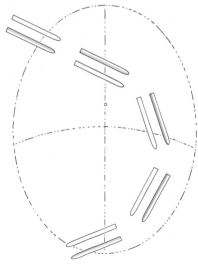

3 As your skis pass over the crest of the mogul, steer them towards the fall line and roll them onto their inside edges.

4 Complete your turn in a controlled, parallel skid down the far side of the mogul.

5 As you finish the turn, rise back up into the standard traverse stance. Look ahead to select a spot for your next turn.

Use terrain parallels to attack moguls with style.

13 · SHORT-RADIUS TURNS

Part of the key to advanced skiing is versatility: having a large assortment of
different techniques to deal with differing conditions.
You can now build on your basic parallel turns to provide yourself with a
short-radius turn for narrow or steep slopes.

By the end of this chapter you should be able to hug the fall line,
performing linked short swings, one turn flowing into the next.

THE DOWNHILL STEM TURN

SPEEDING UP THE START OF YOUR TURN

Short-radius or short-swing turns involve turning your skis quickly, and that means very pronounced un-weighting. One way to perform such exaggerated unweighting would be practically to jump off the snow. A far more effective method is to master rebound unweighting (see page 129), which uses your edges and forward momentum to provide the power. Not only is this less effort, but it also allows you to introduce a strong rhythm into your skiing, as you use the end of each turn to drive the next initiation.

The downhill stem is the best way to learn rebound unweighting. It may seem frustrating at first to go back to stem turns, but downhill stems will help you quickly to get a feel for the short, sharp use of your edges that will open the door to parallel short-swing turns later.

Even when you have moved on, you may still find a use for downhill stems: when you need a little extra stability in the moguls, or when you need to lose

a little speed coming into a turn, you can always put in a quick downhill stem. It is a good safe turn for steep terrain, or if you are carrying a rucksack. This may not be the Ferrari of turns, but if you need a Jeep, this is it.

Unsurprisingly, you start the downhill stem turn by pushing your downhill ski into a stem. The ski slides out smoothly until the edge bites and it seems to stop dead momentarily. This is called checking; the point at which your ski grips is called a platform, as it provides a solid base against which you can push. As your momentum carries your weight forwards and up from your skis, you plant your pole and initiate the turn. It is completed, as usual, with a controlled, parallel skid.

TIPS

■ When you first attempt downhill stem turns, it may be unclear what is meant by a platform. Keep your downhill ski flat on the snow as you slide it out, applying its edge sharply only once it is stemmed. The resulting sharp check should leave you in no doubt.
■ Even while your downhill ski is in the stem position, keep your uphill ski tracking smoothly. It should have very little pressure on it at this stage of the turn.

Alberto Tomba still finds a use for a strong downhill stem.

EXERCISES

■ Practise forming platforms while traversing across an uncrowded slope (see left). As you traverse, flex down, release the edge of your downhill ski and push it into a stem; plant your pole as you feel the edge bite and rebound off the resulting platform. Can you feel the weight come up off your feet? Keep your uphill ski unweighted and tracking straight across the slope throughout. Perform half a dozen traverse platforms as you cross the slope, followed by a downhill stem turn.
■ Try linking your downhill stem turns. As you finish each turn in a flexed position, with pressure on your downhill ski, push it straight out into the stem for the next turn. You should be able to get into a rhythm: stem and plant, up and turn; stem and plant, up and turn.

The traverse platform exercise
Start in a traverse (A), slide your downhill ski into a stem (B), let the edge bite and plant your pole (C). Rebound (D) and return to the traverse stance ready to repeat (E). Keep your uphill ski tracking straight ahead throughout.

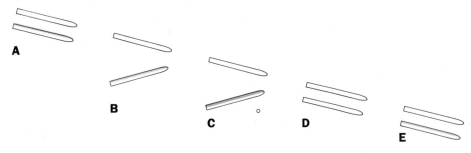

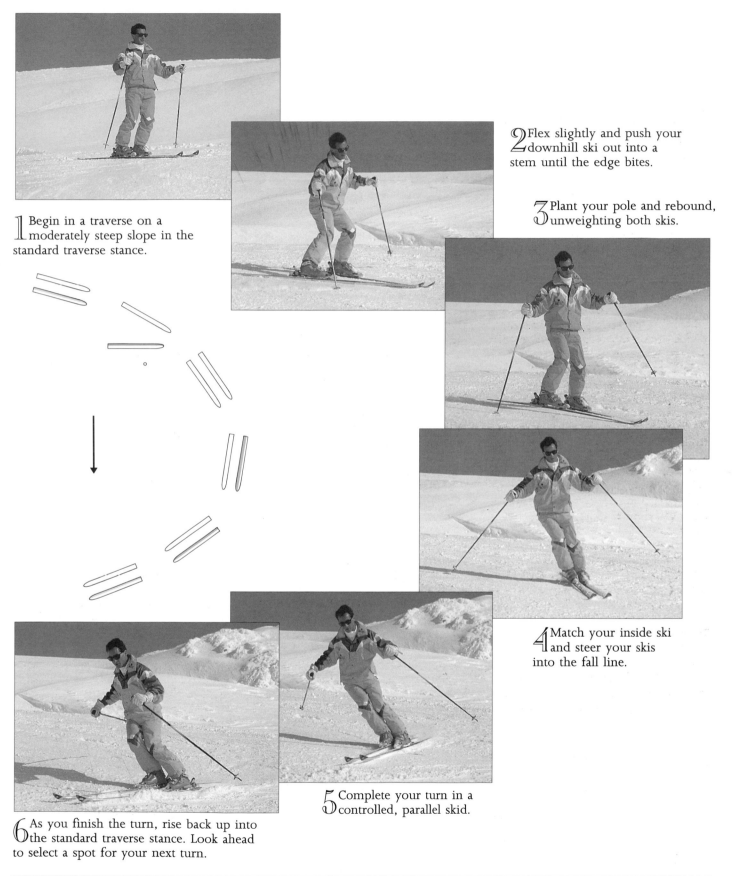

1 Begin in a traverse on a moderately steep slope in the standard traverse stance.

2 Flex slightly and push your downhill ski out into a stem until the edge bites.

3 Plant your pole and rebound, unweighting both skis.

4 Match your inside ski and steer your skis into the fall line.

5 Complete your turn in a controlled, parallel skid.

6 As you finish the turn, rise back up into the standard traverse stance. Look ahead to select a spot for your next turn.

THE PRE-TURN

SPEEDING UP THE START OF YOUR PARALLEL TURN

You are now ready to introduce rebound unweighting into your parallel skiing. The mechanism for achieving this is called a pre-turn. This is a quick, aggressive swing to the hill (see page 124), which sets your downhill ski's edge and provides the power for rebound unweighting. A pre-turn also serves to introduce anticipation into your skiing (see below).

The pre-turn parallel is a direct development of the skills you have learnt in the downhill stem turn: the only difference is that the skis remain parallel throughout, with the uphill ski shadowing the edge set of the downhill ski.

TIP

■ The sharper and more aggressive the pre-turn check, the more effective the rebound unweighting.

ANTICIPATION AND COUNTER-ROTATION

Anticipation

Anticipation is a powerful technique for making the initiation of your turns quicker and more balanced. A simple analogy is that of your body as a spring. When you anticipate, your shoulders and upper body face down the fall line, committed to the turn, while the pressure on your edges keeps your skis and hips tracking across the fall line. This puts your body under torsion, tightening the muscles of your abdomen.

The moment you plant your pole and unweight your skis, the spring unwinds to relieve this muscular tension, steering your skis towards the fall line and initiating your turn. A critical ingredient of this is the pole plant, which times the unweighting and helps you to balance.

Counter-rotation

If anticipation consists of winding up the body's spring and using its release to initiate your turns, counter-rotation takes this one step further. You actually use the muscles of your abdomen to inject power into your steering. This means rotating your skis strongly one way, while your upper body rotates the other way to compensate (hence the name).

Make sure that you don't overdo it. It is easy to fall into the habit of unweighting and throwing your skis around by counter-rotating every turn. This is ugly and tiring, and hinders progress.

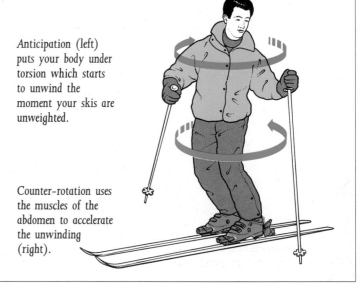

Anticipation (left) puts your body under torsion which starts to unwind the moment your skis are unweighted.

Counter-rotation uses the muscles of the abdomen to accelerate the unwinding (right).

1 Start in the standard traverse stance.

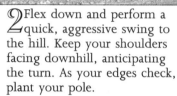

2 Flex down and perform a quick, aggressive swing to the hill. Keep your shoulders facing downhill, anticipating the turn. As your edges check, plant your pole.

3 Rebound and begin your turn, rolling your skis onto their inside edges and into the fall line.

4 Continue to turn in a controlled, parallel skid. Keep the pressure firmly over your outside ski.

5 As you complete the turn look ahead and anticipate your next pre-turn.

The Short-swing Turn

LINKING SHORT-RADIUS TURNS

Once you have mastered the use of the pre-turn to inject rebound unweighting into your parallel turns, the time has come to try short-swings, the ultimate short-radius turns.

Short-swing turns are a very dynamic way of skiing the fall line. Taken to the extreme, your body from the waist up moves exactly down the fall line, while your legs turn under you, providing resistance and control. This type of turn is also called a knee-crossover turn, because it feels as though you are whipping your knees rapidly from side to side under you.

Start with a pre-turn parallel and as you finish each turn, allow your skis to skid into another edge set. You should be able to hit an easy rhythm: check and turn; check and turn. Once you are comfortable with the rhythm, speed up the turns, by setting a stronger edge and rebounding earlier.

(see page 90, on your motor memory)

TIPS

- Vary the amount of force you use on your edges with the type of slope: a steep slope requires a powerful edge set; a shallow slope requires less, and can be skied more smoothly.
- When you rebound from the edge set, project your weight forwards as well as up, especially on steeper slopes. This stops you getting thrown back on the tails of your skis.
- Rhythm is everything.

VISUALIZATION

As your skiing becomes increasingly dynamic, you can no longer simulate it in the comfort of your home, as you could with the earlier moves (see page 90, on your motor memory). The solution is to use visualization.

Visualization involves running through a sequence of movements in your mind, imagining what it would feel like to perform them for real. It is as though, during your skiing, your unconscious mind has built a 'skiing simulator' that you can use to try out new techniques.

Top athletes use visualization in two ways. Firstly they use it to learn new movements: running through them countless times and preparing themselves for the sensations they will feel when they perform the movements for real. Secondly, they use visualization to prepare for competitions: imagining the upcoming event in detail – the location, the noise of the crowd, the nervousness – so that there will be no surprises on the day.

You too can use visualization in these ways. In order to help you to master individual techniques run through them a few times in the evening before trying them on the mountain the next day. Or use visualization to help you prepare for your personal 'competition run', perhaps a new slope you have not yet dared to ski.

Make sure that you are relaxed

In order to visualize effectively, your body must be relaxed, and your mind focused. So always begin with a relaxation session. As you become more adept at visualization you can cut this to a minimum. Initially, however, don't skimp on this part.

- Lie down, or sit in a comfortable arm chair. Breathe deeply and evenly.
- Concentrate on one muscle group at a time, tensing and relaxing it to eliminate any tension. Work outwards from your trunk to your extremities until you are fully relaxed.

Visualize the chosen movement sequence

If you are visualizing a new technique, try to imagine yourself undergoing the full experience. In addition to running through the movements of your chosen technique, try to feel the forces on your body, especially the pressure on your feet.

When visualizing a 'competition run', once again try to replicate the full experience. What does the slope look like as you stand at the top? How steep is it? Does it have moguls? Is anyone watching from the chair lift? Visualize how you feel as you look at the slope.

Push off and start skiing. Focus on your movements, feeling the forces on your body and the rhythm of your turns. Keep looking ahead to plan your route. Seeing yourself mentally negotiate the run well is tremendously powerful in dealing with fear or a lack of self-confidence.

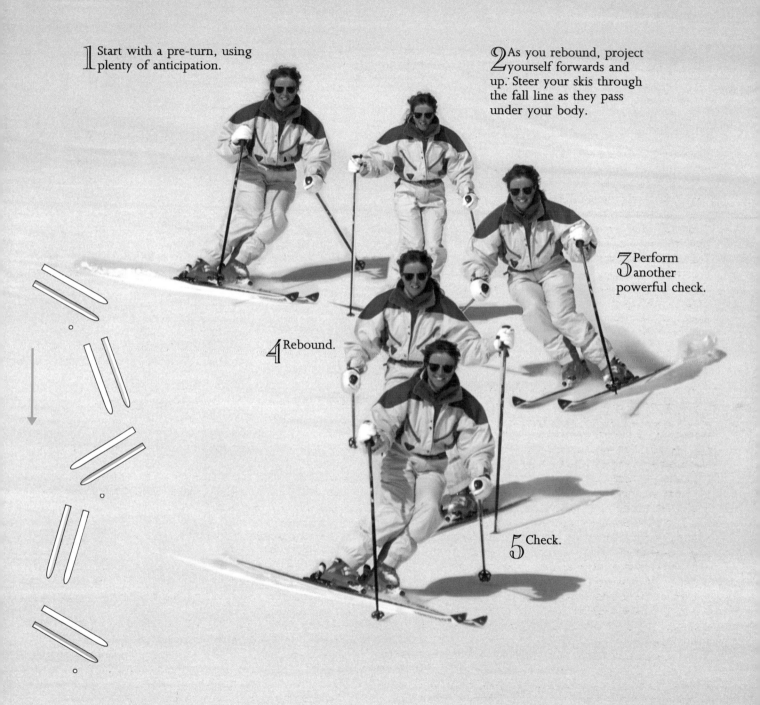

1 Start with a pre-turn, using plenty of anticipation.

2 As you rebound, project yourself forwards and up. Steer your skis through the fall line as they pass under your body.

3 Perform another powerful check.

4 Rebound.

5 Check.

JUMPING

As your skiing becomes more dynamic, you may feel the urge to become airborne. Jumping can be a lot of fun. With the right take off and landing, very little effort is required to 'get air'. Jumps can be very spectacular and they make for great photographs, particularly if you can be silhouetted against a perfect blue sky.

Only experience builds the kind of balance exhibited by competitive freestyle skiers, but don't be afraid to give it a go.

3 Extend vigorously, or 'pop', as you ride up the jump, so that your body is straight as you pass over the lip.

2 Flex slightly to prepare for take off.

1 Approach the jump in the basic stance. Look ahead and spot the lip of the jump.

SAFETY IN THE AIR

Jumping need not be dangerous, as long as you follow some basic safety rules.
- Never jump unless you know the landing is clear.
- Never jump if you are not physically, mentally and technically ready.
- On an unfamiliar jump, start by jumping small, then progressively add speed and height.
- Avoid flat landings.
- Make sure that your bindings are sufficiently tight.
- Never attempt somersaults, or inverted aerials, without expert supervision: there are plenty of freestyle clubs or camps that would be only too happy to teach you these moves safely.

4 Remain relaxed but compact in the air.

5 Spot your landing and return to the extended position with your skis parallel to the snow.

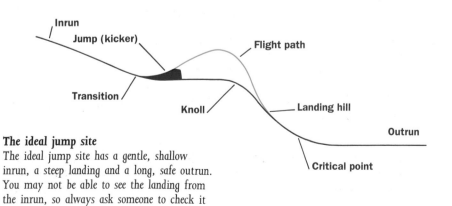

The ideal jump site

The ideal jump site has a gentle, shallow inrun, a steep landing and a long, safe outrun. You may not be able to see the landing from the inrun, so always ask someone to check it is safe to jump.

Inrun

Jump (kicker)

Flight path

Transition

Knoll

Landing hill

Outrun

Critical point

6 Absorb the impact on landing by allowing your legs to flex. Push your arms forwards to keep your weight over the centre of your skis as you ski away.

SHAPES

Once you have mastered the basic jump, try some different shapes. Start with a Spread Eagle or a Tip Drop, and then get more adventurous. (For more advanced shapes, see pages 169-170.)

Spread Eagle (right), Twister (below), Tip Drop (below right) and Mule Kick (opposite).

14 · LONG-RADIUS TURNS

You have seen the real experts charging down the slopes at two or three times your speed. They look relaxed and confident, and the worst of it is, they don't even look like they are exerting much effort as they clock up their skiing miles! What is preventing you from skiing like this?

High-speed Cruising

BUILDING SPEED AND CONTROL

Long-radius turns, also called giant-slalom turns, present perhaps the greatest technical challenge on the slopes. You have plenty of time for each turn, but only supreme control produces the slow, accurate movements required. The key lies in letting your skis do the work for you, using their design to carve your turns. You must improve the precision with which you steer your skis, as well as your balance and feel for the forces on your edges.

Each stage of the turn is involved: at the initiation, you must avoid over-steering your skis into a skid; in the middle of the turn, you must match the turning radius to the forces on your skis; and at the end of the turn, you must control the tendency of the backs of your skis to break into a skid. If you can improve your long-radius turns, you will see the pay-off in all your skiing.

At this point, a word of warning. You are about to tackle the world of advanced skiing; you can no longer expect to make breakthroughs at the same heady pace as when you first began to ski. But improvement is still possible, and every small advance now will reap a large reward if you persevere and enjoy the challenge.

It is also worth noting that no two people have exactly the same build, and no two people have exactly the same attitude to their skiing. So it follows that no two people should ski in exactly the same way. The more advanced your skiing becomes, the less you should try to look like everyone else, and the more you should concentrate on developing your own individual style.

Don't try to integrate all the techniques described here simultaneously into every turn. Instead, experiment with each of them, building aspects into your skiing if you find them helpful. Let yourself be guided by three feelings: power, precision and relaxation.

Power
You are using your skis, muscles and gravity in harmony: you are aware of strong forces during your turns, but they are all centred on your edges and your body is dynamically balanced to resist them easily.

Precision
Your skis follow exactly the path you steer, producing smooth, rounded turns that are not thrown off by irregularities in the snow. Your body too is totally precise in its movements, with no loss of balance or unnecessary overcompensation.

Relaxation
You are focused on two things: the terrain ahead and the feeling of your skiing. The essential muscles are tensed momentarily (but never cramped) during each turn, while muscles not involved in the turn are relaxed, ready to respond if they are required for balance.

HOW LONG IS A SKI?

As you begin to experiment with turns at higher speeds, you may want to use a longer pair of skis. A longer ski provides greater stability and holds its edge more easily than a shorter one. The ideal for high-speed cruising is a giant-slalom ski, around 30-40 cm longer than your height.

But take care when choosing a cruising ski: you must be able to bend it in order to carve your turns, so it mustn't be too stiff for your weight or athletic ability. Remember that most ski shops let you test skis, so take advantage of this to try a few pairs of skis and find one that suits your cruising style best.

CARVING

LETTING YOUR SKIS DO THE WORK

Most intermediate skiers are not comfortable when their skis point down the fall line because of the rapid acceleration that results. They turn their skis as quickly as possible across the fall line, usually so quickly that they break into a skidded turn. There is nothing wrong with this: it is an entirely appropriate, straightforward way to lose excessive speed, and the one that has been recommended so far throughout this book.

Balancing against a skidding edge like this, however, requires concentration and effort, limiting the speed at which you can react to the terrain. In a carved turn, on the other hand, this skidding is eliminated. Your outside ski is bent into reverse camber. This, together with the ski's side-cut, defines the exact radius of the turn being performed. You do not have to exert any rotational force on your skis: balancing against the forces of the turn is sufficient to keep the ski running as though on rails.

No turn is ever 100% carved, despite the best efforts of skiers and ski manufacturers. The shorter the radius of the turn, the harder it is to achieve the extreme bend of the ski that would be required to match the radius, and hence the more skidding creeps into the turn.

The design of their skis allows racers to carve their turns to conserve speed or even accelerate through the gates (above). The same design enables recreational skiers to cruise with speed and confidence (below).

Why does a carving ski turn?

In a carved turn, your ski is bent into reverse camber. The radius of the edge exactly matches that of the turn, and the ski does not skid at all (compare with the skidding ski, page 100).

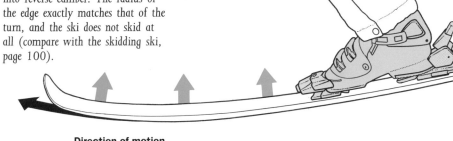

Resistance of snow distributed over entire edge

Ski bent into reverse camber

Direction of motion

Carved turns

In a carved turn, the skis slide cleanly, throwing up little or no snow. A carved turn results in a narrow track, showing how the edge has been set against the snow.

Skidded turns

If you skid a turn, you throw up a plume of snow. A skidded turn results in a wide track as the ski moves sideways across the snow.

The Beginning of the Turn

ELIMINATING OVER-STEERING

Most intermediate skiers initiate their turns on the flat by steering their skis strongly. Most also become used to relying on unweighting to facilitate this strong steering action. But once your skis break into a skid, it is almost impossible to arrest them. For a strong, carved turn, you need a different type of initiation, to reduce the amount of effort you put into steering your skis at the start of the turn.

EARLY PRESSURE TRANSFER

Transferring pressure to the outside ski very early in the turn makes it almost impossible for you to over-steer your skis. Try this experiment on a very shallow slope. As you finish a turn across the fall line, plant your pole and lift your downhill ski off the snow. Don't do anything else. Let your body drop down the fall line without the support of your downhill ski, crossing over from above to below your skis. The pressure moves to the inside edge of your uphill ski, causing it to turn into the fall line and then back under you, preventing potential disaster.

Don't use any up- or down-motion at this point: stay flexed throughout the initiation of the turn so that you don't interfere with the ski's natural tendency to turn. It is very important to try this on a shallow slope, one that you can normally ski without any difficulty. It requires a lot of faith to believe that your skis will respond and turn under you. If you are worried by the steepness of the slope, it is quite likely you will retreat into your normal unweight-and-swivel initiation.

DYNAMIC CARVED INITIATION

You have seen how to prevent yourself from over-steering the beginning of your turns by transferring the pressure early off your downhill ski. But if you try this on steeper slopes, you end up accelerating down the fall line while you wait for your skis to come round. You need to add some power to your turn initiations in order to speed up the turn.

Instead of staying flexed throughout the turn initiation, try extending your uphill leg as the pressure comes onto it. At the same time, project your body forwards and down the fall line. This achieves two things. Firstly, you speed up the crossover of your body from above to below your skis, rolling them quickly onto their new edges. Secondly, by pushing down powerfully on your uphill ski you add to its reverse camber (the opposite of unweighting). The combination of these two effects results in a quicker initiation to your turn.

TIP

■ Make sure that you are not extending until the pressure is on your uphill ski. Otherwise you are probably still unweighting and over-steering.

If your weight is too far back at the initiation of the turn, you may find your skis unwilling to co-operate.

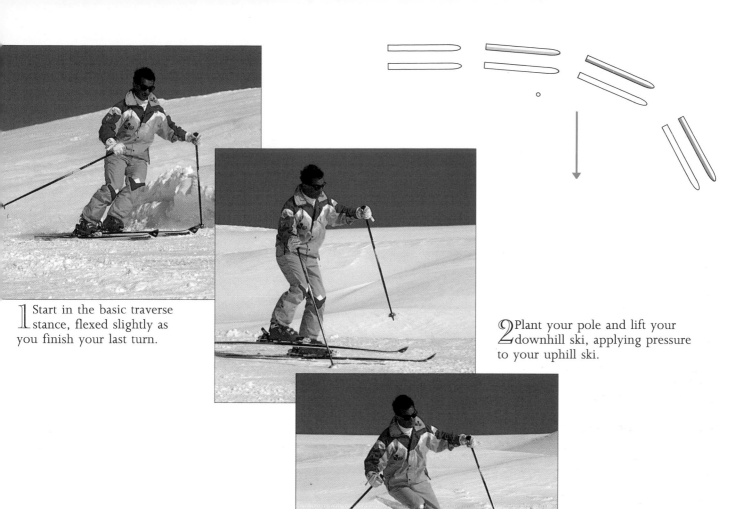

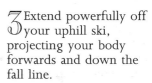

1 Start in the basic traverse stance, flexed slightly as you finish your last turn.

2 Plant your pole and lift your downhill ski, applying pressure to your uphill ski.

3 Extend powerfully off your uphill ski, projecting your body forwards and down the fall line.

4 Keep the pressure firmly on your outside ski as it turns into the fall line.

You will occasionally spot racers take a step uphill as they transfer their weight on to their uphill ski. They are adjusting their line to allow themselves a longer turning radius between the gates and thus to carry more speed.

You may even spot a so-called scissor step turn, in which the racer's skis diverge at the moment of the weight transfer. This acts like a skating step, allowing the racer to push out onto the new ski, accelerating into the next turn.

The scissor step turn. The great Pirmin Zurbriggen is about to step out aggressively onto his uphill ski, adjusting his line to take the next gate straighter, and using the opportunity to accelerate with a skating step.

You can try the step turn for yourself next time you go for a fast cruise. It is a dynamic turn and can be especially useful in breaking the habit of skiing with your feet locked together.

THE MIDDLE OF THE TURN

ADDING POWER AND PRECISION

Once you feel that you have mastered a carved initiation to your turns, it is time to add power to the middle of your turns.

APPLYING PRESSURE TO ONE SKI

In order to maintain your carve throughout the turn, you must be skiing with all your weight on the outside ski throughout the turn. You have heard this advice before; now you need to be absolutely strict with yourself. Every turn must be performed with pressure on just one ski.

The reason for this is that unless you ski at exceptionally high speeds, you have only enough force at your disposal to bend one ski into reverse camber. Distributing the pressure over both skis dissipates this force, leaving your skis too straight and forcing you to retreat into a skid.

You don't need to lift your inside ski high off the snow; most expert skiers actually allow it to brush across the surface. This way they concentrate the maximum force on their outside ski without performing any excess movements. It also provides an added bonus: a brief, welcome moment of relaxation for the unweighted inside leg. This prevents you from becoming tired and contributes significantly to the fluidity of your skiing.

If you want to master fast, effortless cruising, you have to get used to putting all your weight on your outside ski.

MATCHING THE RADII OF SKI AND TURN

Now that you are skiing with all your weight on your outside ski, the challenge is to match the radius described by its edge to that of your turn.

You are familiar with the fact that your ski is narrower at the middle than at the tip or tail. Imagine placing your ski on a flat surface; now tilt it slightly onto one of its edges and push down over the bindings. It bends until its waist touches the surface; the ski describes a gentle arc. Tilt the ski more aggressively on its side and the arc described becomes more pronounced. So the more you set your skis on edge, the sharper the radius of turn your skis will want to produce.

But this is only part of the story. Even more important in determining the radius described by your outside ski is the amount of force you use to put it into reverse camber. On a yielding surface, such as snow, for any given angle of edge set, the harder you push down, the more your ski bends and the tighter the radius of turn it will produce.

So now you have two adjustments to help you to match your ski radius to that of your turn: more or less edge, and more or less force. If you can co-ordinate their action, your skis will carve and you will tap into an incredible surge of power in the middle of your turn. The key to this is to increase the amount of hip angulation (see page 126) that you use.

TIPS

■ Choose a groomed, easy slope that you feel comfortable skiing at fairly high speed.
■ Feel your skis moving out from under you as your hips drop to the inside of the turn.
■ It should feel as though your outside ski is on rails, and all you are doing is balancing against it. Settle on the desired speed and radius of turn first, then experiment with different amounts of angulation until you achieve this feeling.
■ If it doesn't click, you may not be using enough speed. Make sure that the slope you have chosen is clear, then pump up the volume.

1 As you finish each turn look ahead and anticipate the next.

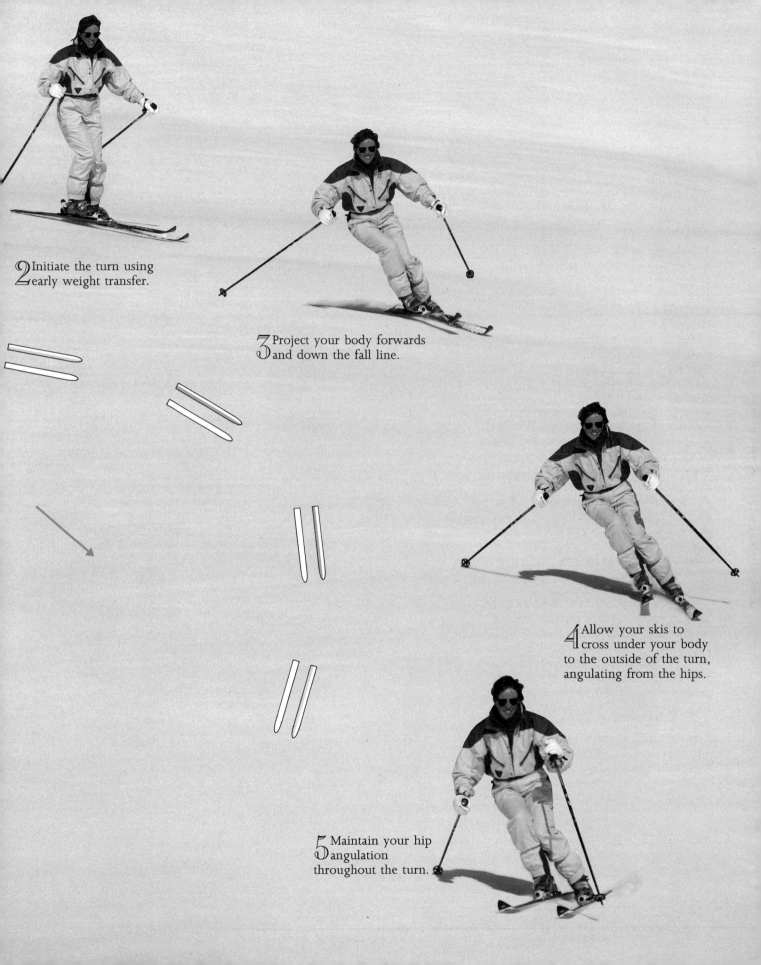

2 Initiate the turn using early weight transfer.

3 Project your body forwards and down the fall line.

4 Allow your skis to cross under your body to the outside of the turn, angulating from the hips.

5 Maintain your hip angulation throughout the turn.

CONTROLLING YOUR SPEED

Part of the key to the relaxed charge of the expert skier lies in reading and responding to the slope. The next time you watch an expert skier in action, look for the tell-tale signs: expert skiers tighten their turns as the slope steepens, lengthen them as it flattens out, adjusting their position on the slope constantly and subtly to give themselves the most flowing line.

It is this ability to use the slope, as much as the quality of the turns themselves, that sets apart the truly expert from the simply advanced skier. Achieving this symphony of resistance and flow requires experience. But it also requires the ability to control your speed without reverting to skidding your turns.

Shortening the radius of the turn
One way to control your speed is to shorten the radius of your turns. You have already seen how the more your ski is edged and put into reverse camber, the tighter the radius of turn it will produce (see page 154). Your skis are also designed to help you to alter the radius of your turn in another way: the fronts of your skis are softer than the backs, and the tip wider than the tail. The result? The further forwards you apply pressure during a turn, the shorter its radius will be. Pushing your knee forwards and into the turn applies your weight to the softer front of the ski, producing a shorter-radius carved turn.

Modifying your path
You can also control your speed by modifying the path taken by your skis. The easiest way is to hold on to your turns for longer, bringing you further out of the fall line on each turn. Alternatively, introducing more angulation, you can project your skis further from the axis of each turn so that they have further to travel.

Speed control in carved turns

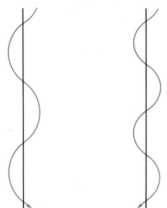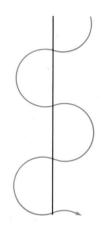

In order to control your speed when cruising...

...you can either shorten the radius of your turns...

...project your skis further from the fall line using more angulation...

...or hold on to each turn for longer.

Starting with a long-radius turn...

...tighten the radius by pushing your outside knee forwards and towards the inside of the turn.

The End of the Turn

KEEPING THE POWER ON

The tendency for your skis to break into a skid is at its greatest at the end of the turn. At this point, centrifugal force and gravity act together to pull you directly down the fall line. That is why so many turns that start by carving end up in a frustrating skid. There are two techniques that can help to prevent this: pressuring the back of your skis and foot drive.

PRESSURING THE BACK OF YOUR SKIS

The first technique for beefing up the ends of your turns is to apply more pressure to the tails of your skis. It is always the back of the ski that breaks away first at the end of a turn if you overload your ski. As you finish your turn, let your weight move progressively back until you are pushing vertically down through your outside heel. This lets the back of the ski determine the radius of the turn and prevents it from skidding out.

FOOT DRIVE

A second and related technique is a powerful and versatile one called foot drive. It can solve even a very ingrained problem at the end of your turns, and can be used to gain extra purchase on hard, icy surfaces. The trick lies in pushing your outside foot forwards as you complete your turn. This slices your edge into the snow and shifts the pressure onto the tails. The trick lies in then projecting your body forwards sufficiently during the following initiation so that you regain your balance over your skis.

THE JET TURN

In the seventies the young Ingemar Stenmark shot to international success and fame, courtesy of the jet turn. The skis are jetted forwards out of the turn in a type of extreme foot drive. At the time, it was the fastest way to get through the gates.

Ingemar Stenmark, the father of the jet turn.

Take your normal high-speed cruising turn...

...and use foot drive to make your skis stick like glue at the end of the turn.

THE AERIAL TURN

If you are looking for new thrills in your high speed cruising, try initiating your turns in the air! As you finish each turn, project yourself off any small bump, turn and land on the inside edge of your uphill ski.

Add extra excitement to high-speed cruising with the aerial turn.

15 · FALL-LINE MOGUL SKIING

Every good bumps run in the world breeds its own little clique of initiates. These are expert mogul skiers, who hug the fall line where normal skiers are forced into desperate traverses; absorb bumps that throw others into the air; and, most annoying of all, seem to be enjoying themselves. What is their secret?

Unfortunately, there is no single answer. Fall-line mogul skiing requires a reasonable level of strength and fitness, sound basic technique and good balance. Some specialized techniques will enable you to cope with the terrain as you perform your turns. But equally importantly, you need the ability to read the slope: expert mogul skiing depends on recognizing patterns in the moguls and responding quickly. It is this path-finding skill, rather than any technique, that can be most difficult to master.

In previous chapters, you have learnt how to cope with moguls; the emphasis has been more on survival than enjoyment. This chapter introduces fall-line mogul skiing. And the real secret to mastering the bumps? Get out there and ski them!

ABSORPTION

SMOOTHING OUT THE BUMPS

As you approach the crest of each mogul, intense pressure builds under your skis. When they pass over the mogul, this pressure is released and your skis may even lose contact with the snow. This causes great difficulty as you try to turn and control your speed. The solution lies in absorption.

By allowing your legs to flex under you as you ski over each mogul, you are reducing the pressure between your skis and the snow. Once your skis have passed over the crest, extend your legs strongly, maintaining contact with the snow.

EXERCISE

Practise this next time you find yourself in an easy mogul field with a good safe run-out area. As you reach the last few bumps, let your skis run straight down the fall line. Keep your head and upper body calm while using your legs to smooth out the moguls. Allowing the moguls to flex your legs is fine, but you need to push down actively into the troughs to keep your skis on the snow. Notice how the force on your skis is also smoothed out.

Another good way to practise this is to traverse at a moderate speed or per-

form giant slalom turns through a mogul field (making sure first, of course, that the path is clear). Keep your upper body from rising and falling as you pass over the moguls, and push your arms forwards as you absorb the bumps.

TIP

■ Your upper body must remain calm and facing the fall line throughout, letting your legs absorb the mogul under you. Don't let yourself fold forwards from the waist.

As you hit each mogul use your hips, knees and ankles to absorb it and keep your arms in front of you at all times. Your centre of mass should follow a straight line.

The Compression Turn

TURNING IN THE MOGULS

Once you feel comfortable absorbing moguls by flexing and re-extending your legs, you are ready to use this in a turn, called a compression turn. Try it first on an isolated mogul.

TIP

■ Keep your arms in front of you at all times. Plant and release your pole as far as possible using only wrist action.

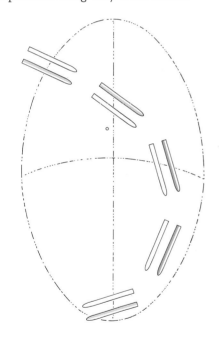

1 Approach the chosen mogul.

2 As your skis ride up the mogul, allow your legs to flex and plant your pole on the top.

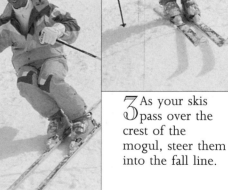

3 As your skis pass over the crest of the mogul, steer them into the fall line.

4 Extend your legs actively to keep your skis in contact with the snow.

5 Finish the turn in the normal stance.

PATH FINDING

LEARNING TO USE THE MOGULS

Compression turns help to smooth out the effects of violent rises and falls in the terrain, and are a valuable addition to your skier's tool-kit. But on their own, they will not transform your bump skiing: you also need to modify your path through the moguls.

As you pass over the crest of a bump, there is a limit to the power with which you can re-extend. You cannot guarantee that your edges will work effectively on the downhill side of every mogul. All too often, you end up in an uncontrollable skid into the trough. You must learn instead to stay off your edges on the flank of the mogul, turning only when the terrain provides you with something against which to bank your skis.

ELIMINATING THE SIDESLIP

In order to ski this route, first learn to check your speed against the front of a mogul. Select a mogul on an easy slope and perform a pre-turn (see page 138) against its uphill side, planting your pole on its crest. Progressively exaggerate the pre-turn until you are checking strongly on the front of the bump.

Once you have your speed under control, try letting your skis point straight downhill as they pass over the crest of the mogul. Don't steer, just relax and let them accelerate. Only when you reach the front of the next mogul, and the terrain comes up to meet you, do you steer your skis into another quick check. Repeat the whole process and get into a rhythm: check and run; check and run.

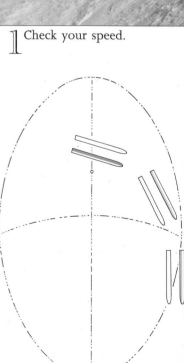

1 Check your speed.

2 Point your skis downhill.

3 Let your skis run.

Any mogul slope with a large number of good skiers should develop regular moguls with obvious lines to ski.

5 Finish your turn strongly on this mogul, and anticipate the next.

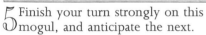

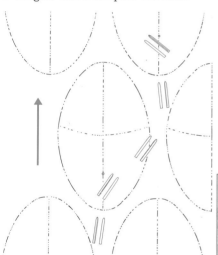

4 Steer your skis through a rounded turn towards the front of the next mogul.

3 Let your skis run towards the fall line.

2 Check smoothly and powerfully on the first mogul.

1 Look ahead and plan your turn.

ROUNDING OUT YOUR TURNS

Once you have eliminated the sideslip, you are only a short step from 'real' fall-line mogul skiing. Follow the same line, but round out your turns by checking less abruptly, against the sides, rather than the fronts of the moguls.

POLE PLANTING IN THE MOGULS

THE KEY TO GOOD BALANCE

Your pole plant is even more important in mogul skiing than when skiing the flat. Any fault in your pole plant is instantly transmitted to your body, resulting in a loss of balance and control. Work on improving your pole plants and your mogul skiing will improve dramatically. Never leave your pole planted too long or it will throw your weight back onto the tails of your skis. If problems persist, try using a shorter pair of poles for skiing bumps.

1 Plant your pole early and further down the fall line than usual.

2 Keep your arms forwards.

3 Allow your pole to release as you pass over the mogul.

The Mother of all Mogul Fields.

JUST WEIGHT AND SKI

If you watch talented skiers in the moguls, at times they appear to let their weight drop back on to the tails of their skis. This is an illusion: the force on their skis always acts straight up through their feet.

The secret lies in the braking that occurs each time you absorb a mogul. It is like standing in a train as it slows down: you lean back, but the deceleration keeps your weight squarely over your feet. If you don't get it right, you topple forwards. Similarly, when you absorb a mogul, your skis slow down. For your weight to continue to act through your feet your centre of gravity must be behind them or you will be thrown forwards from the waist.

Once your skis have passed over the crest of the mogul, however, they are no longer braking. Your weight must once again be forward. (If you continue to lean back once the train has stopped, you fall over.) To avoid being thrown back onto your tails at this point, keep your arms in front as you absorb the mogul.

Perfect balance means allowing your centre of mass to drop back as you absorb a mogul, to balance your deceleration.

SPEED CONTROL

FINDING THE BRAKES

You should quickly master fall line mogul skiing in easy bump fields. When the slopes become steeper, however, you may find speed control a problem. One way to deal with this is to skid into more powerful checks (this should feel similar to performing short-swing turns, see page 140). An alternative technique is to modify your path through the bumps, either by turning every second bump or by steering your skis further from the fall line each turn.

Even many expert skiers have difficulty in picking their path through a mogul field. That is why you often hear excuses about skis being too long for the moguls. Remember the following points:

■ Use the fronts of the moguls. Let your skis bank against the bump as you finish the turn, instead of skidding down the flank on your edges.

■ If you lose your rhythm, point your tips down the fall line to the front of the next mogul, where you can check your speed.

■ Look ahead. You should always have a general idea of your route through a mogul field before you push off. Plan the first four or five turns, then keep looking ahead at least one or two turns.

Look ahead, not at your skis!

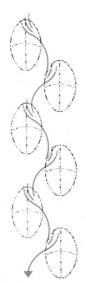

The ideal route is direct and fast.

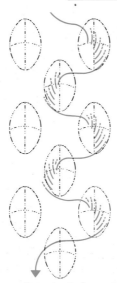

If it's too fast, absorb the moguls and skid down their flanks.

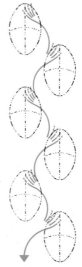

Alternatively, skid into more powerful checks...

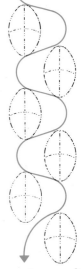

...or try steering your skis further from the fall line each turn.

Advanced Techniques

DEALING WITH THE ROGUE MOGUL

Once in a while, every self-respecting mogul run will throw at you a bump so deformed that it defies the usual techniques. The best plan is to change lines to avoid these maverick moguls. Often, however, you are on them too quickly. This is where three special techniques come in: a foot thrust or a pre-jump can help you to negotiate moguls that sit across your line like park benches; hip projection gets your skis back on the snow after you have absorbed particularly big bumps.

Foot thrust
If you see a particularly steep mogul coming, push your feet forwards to anticipate the impact. This will prevent you from folding from the waist.

The pre-jump
If you think even foot thrust will not keep you from being thrown forwards by a mogul, you have no choice: a pre-jump is hard work, but it does get you out of trouble. As the mogul approaches, jump, lifting your ski tips, and land on the front of the mogul.

To avoid this...

...use foot thrust.

To keep your skis on the snow...

If necessary miss the trough altogether and use a pre-jump to land on the front of the next bump.

Hip projection
After absorbing a particularly big mogul, use hip projection to push your tips back down towards the snow. Project your hips forwards while pushing down through the balls of your feet.

...use hip projection.

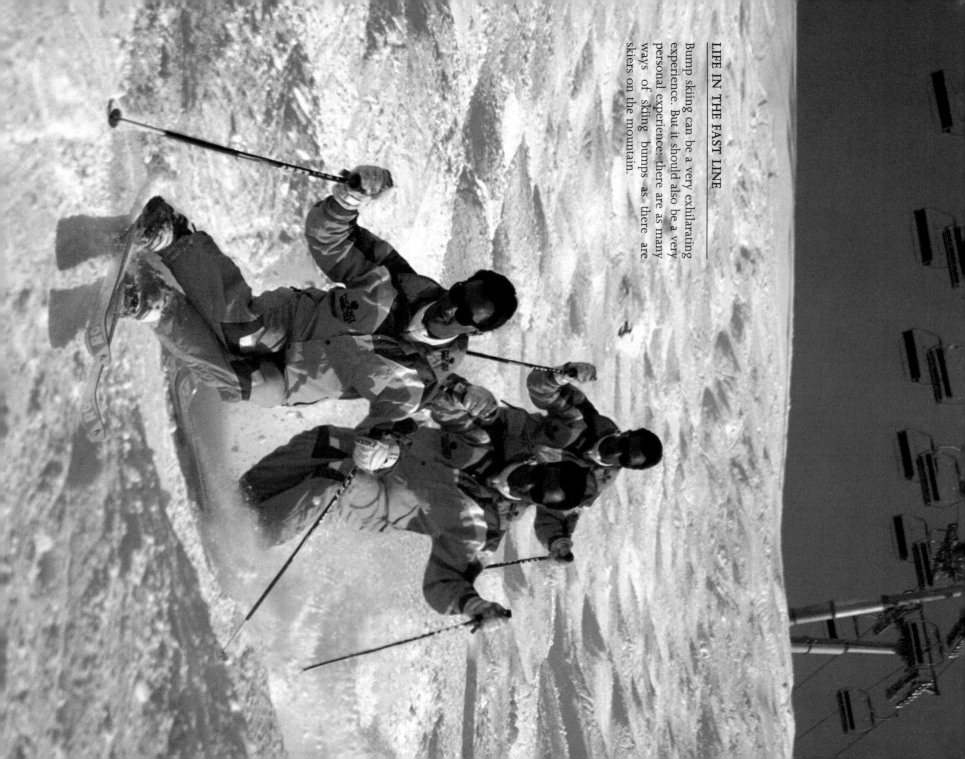

LIFE IN THE FAST LINE

Bump skiing can be a very exhilarating experience. But it should also be a very personal experience: there are as many ways of skiing bumps as there are skiers on the mountain.

ADVANCED JUMPS

As you spend more time in the air, you may want to try some more advanced shapes. The sky's the limit.

Beware: the Backscratcher (right) and Daffy (below) require height to keep your tips off the snow. The Splitster (below right) is similar to a Daffy, but the skis are rotated.

The Helicopter, a 360-degree rotation in the air, requires a little gymnastic ability and a lot of nerve.

16 · OFF-PISTE SKIING

Skiing off piste offers some of the most memorable experiences on snow: the exhilaration of untouched powder, the solitude and beauty of the mountains, and a glowing feeling of self-reliance and achievement. At some point every skier begins to feel limited by the terrain offered by groomed runs, and tempted by the expanses of snow off piste.

Off-piste skiing should never be undertaken without caution and respect for the mountains. While everyone from strong intermediate upwards can enjoy skiing off piste, you must be aware of your limitations, and avoid being over-ambitious. This chapter covers the precautions you should take before leaving the marked runs, and introduces the techniques you will need.

Safety Matters

LEARNING RESPECT FOR THE MOUNTAINS

If you leave the marked pistes, it is assumed that you know what you're doing – and you do it at your own risk.

■ Make sure your insurance policy covers off-piste skiing (see page 214).

■ Never ski off piste alone. Unless you are really familiar with the route, take an experienced guide. Simply following a set of tracks is no guarantee of safety: conditions change rapidly in the mountains, and the author of the tracks may have been a much stronger skier than you – or lost.

■ Before setting out, make sure that you are familiar with the resort and the conditions. Routes alter with the seasons and the weather: an enjoyable gully in February might be a roaring torrent in April.

■ Make sure that you are aware of the level of avalanche danger , and check the weather forecast: being caught off piste in fog or in a blizzard is extremely dangerous.

■ Always let someone know where you are going.

■ Plan your path to avoid walking uphill as much as possible. Learn to read the terrain: gentle dips in the snow could hide streams or even crevasses; suspicious bumps could represent hidden rocks.

■ In certain areas, especially in North America, back-country skiing is restricted in order to protect wilderness nature reserves. If you ignore signs, you risk a heavy fine or the confiscation of your lift pass.

AVALANCHES

The best way to deal with avalanches is never to be caught in one. Knowledge is safety: the more you understand about avalanches and their causes, the better you will be able to avoid risky situations.

The three main types of avalanche are powder, slab and wet snow.

Powder avalanches

These generally start from a single point, widening as they progress. Ever-increasing volumes of powder snow are thrown into the air, flowing down the slope as a dense cloud. Speeds can reach 400kph (250mph), and the shock wave of the approaching avalanche can flatten everything in its path. Although rare, especially in Europe, this type of avalanche is extremely dangerous, battering or choking its victims to death.

A powder avalanche threatens a group of skiers. Note the fracture line from earlier slab avalanches.

A wet snow slide.

Slab avalanches

Around 75% of all avalanche incidents involving skiers are due to slab avalanches. The most common cause is wind: snow is carried over ridges and dropped on lee slopes, building a thick, unstable layer of dense snow, called wind slab. This type of avalanche, however, can occur whenever layers of snow do not cohere strongly, for instance if the intervening surface is smooth, damp or granular.

The reason slab avalanches are so dangerous is that the instability is invisible to the naked eye. It may be buried under a layer of fresh, inviting powder. But given the right trigger, such as the tracks and weight of a skier, the top layers of snow fracture right across the slope and begin to slide over the layers below. Victims find themselves standing on or below the moving slab, with very little chance of escaping as it breaks up and carries them down the slope.

Wet snow avalanches

In spring, or whenever it is subjected to elevated temperatures, snow transforms rapidly (see page 119). As a result its cohesion and strength are reduced: wet snow avalanches frequently result. These generally start from a single point, spreading as they slide. Their progress is usually slow, unless they encounter steeper terrain or are funnelled into a gully. Due to the density of snow carried, these avalanches can be extremely destructive. Once they stop, they set like concrete; buried victims are unable to move or breathe.

Judging avalanche danger

A number of methods have been developed to ascertain the safety of a slope. The most thorough involve digging a hole in a similar (but safe) slope to check if the layers of snow are stable. However, unless you have received specialized training, your hole is unlikely to tell you much. If you plan to do a lot of off-piste skiing, take a course in snow safety, organized by the local guides' associations or ski club.

Meanwhile, look out for the following signs of avalanche danger:
- Steep, open slopes, especially convex.
- Large amounts of new snow – anything over 20cm (about 8in).
- High winds.
- Cornices or other evidence of recent wind activity.
- Explosions or other signs of avalanche clearing on nearby slopes.
- Evidence of recent avalanches on other, similar slopes.
- Cracks in the snow.
- Hollow-sounding snow surface, creaking noises of large masses of snow moving.
- Sounds of dripping water or balls of wet snow running down the slope.

Cornices are formed when snow is deposited on the lee side of a ridge by the wind. They can be tempting, inviting you to break through them from below if small and fresh, or drop off onto a powdery landing if large and overhanging. But never forget that they are dangerous. Even small cornices can consist of many tonnes of snow, and the slopes below them are frequently unstable wind slab. If you have to cross a cornice and you are at all unsure about its ability to hold you, you should be roped up.

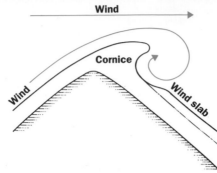

Wind slab
Skiing on or below wind slab is very dangerous. The presence of a cornice is a tell-tale sign of the risk.

Cornices can be fun in fresh snow, but never underestimate their danger.

Reducing the risk of being caught

If you find yourself on a route that you judge to be exposed to avalanche danger, take the following precautions.

■ Cross exposed slopes as early as possible. As a general rule, exposed south-facing slopes should not be attempted after about 11a.m., when the sun has warmed them.

■ Minimize the time spent in exposed locations, such as narrow gullies or obvious chutes where earlier avalanches have destroyed the trees.

■ Plan your path to stick to ridges or valley floors. Take advantage of safer areas, such as among trees and below, rather than above, rocks.

■ Loosen any equipment that you may need to jettison in a hurry (rucksacks, powder straps and poles).

■ Move one by one, with a safe gap between members of the group. Do not assume it is safe because others have traversed successfully. Group members should wait in safety and watch the moving skier.

■ Do not stop on exposed slopes. If you fall, get moving again as quickly as possible. Cleaning your glasses can wait until you reach safety.

If you are caught in an avalanche

Being caught in an avalanche is always serious. Luck plays a large role in survival and there are few hard and fast rules about what to do. The following seem to make sense.

■ Try to ski out, either by out-running the slide, or by escaping to the side.

■ If there is no escape, throw off your skis, poles and rucksack. Try to 'swim' towards the edge, or at least keep yourself on the surface.

■ Grab hold of any fixed object you encounter such as a rock or tree.

■ If you are in danger of being covered in debris, hyper-ventilate and curl up. Protect your mouth and nose with your hands, and keep them there so you have a chance to dig yourself a breathing space as the slide stops.

■ Above all, keep calm and save your air and strength. Shout only when you hear someone within range.

If a companion is caught in an avalanche

Speed is essential. Two-thirds of fatalities are due to suffocation, so the chances of survival diminish very quickly after the first half-hour.

■ Make sure the slope is stable after the initial slide. Stay alert as you search so you are not caught in a second slide.

■ Mark the spot where the victim was last seen.

■ Carry out a quick search first, then a more detailed hunt. Shout and use the handle of your pole or the tail of your ski to probe the snow. Divide the area and search methodically. Most probable areas are at the edges of the slides, or around boulders and trees.

■ If there are several in the group, two should go for help after a first quick search; the rest carry on searching.

■ Once you have located the victim, uncover the face with all speed.

■ Depending on the type of avalanche, injuries are likely to be suffocation or crushing, as well as hypothermia (see page 215).

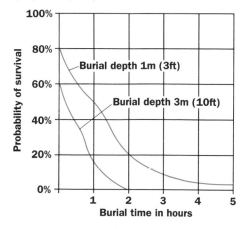

Avalanche survival

Your chance of survival is greatly increased if you are discovered quickly. The deeper you are buried, the worse the situation.

Extra safety equipment is needed for 'serious' off-piste skiing.

Transceivers offer the best chance of rapidly locating buried skiers. These can be hired, and should be supplied by ski guides. They are worn by all members of the party, and are left on the transmit setting throughout the day. They emit a signal at a given frequency (457kHz in Europe, 2275Hz in North America). If one of the party is taken by an avalanche, the rest switch to the receiving mode to locate the incoming signal.

Read the instructions and practise before you need to use your transceiver. Make sure you install new alkaline batteries and wear the unit close to your body where it won't be ripped off in an avalanche. Remember to set it to transmit when you set off, and don't switch it off until you return. If your transceiver is not compatible with that of your colleagues, it is of no use.

Avalanche cords are a poor second. On dangerous-looking slopes, you trail a 10m cord behind you as you ski. If you are buried, part of the cord may remain visible.

Recco transmitters contain a chip of material that can be detected under snow by a receiver. They are cheap and light, and can be attached to your clothing or ski boots. While better than nothing, their disadvantage is that the searchers must be equipped with a receiver. In practice this means waiting for suitably-equipped rescuers.

A **shovel** and **first aid kit** should be carried if your off-piste skiing takes you any great distance from help, as should a **reflecting emergency blanket** (for touring equipment, see page 199).

Using a transceiver
First search down the flow line from the last seen point, following the routes marked.

Single search

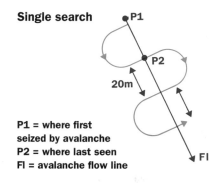

P1 = where first seized by avalanche
P2 = where last seen
Fl = avalanche flow line

Group search

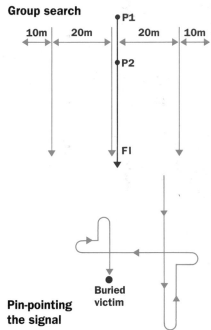

Pin-pointing the signal

Once you have received a signal from the buried transceiver, turn off all except one receiver. Walk in the direction of the signal until you reach the point where the sound is strongest. Turn through 90 degrees and once again find the place where the sound is strongest. Repeat this process until you can pinpoint the buried victim precisely.

POWDER

Powder is the skier's magic word. It is fresh snow that has not yet been skied or affected by sun or warmth. Good powder is dry, creaks when you step on it, hisses when you ski on it, sprays in a fine dust at speed and gives you the experience of a lifetime.

For many skiers, learning to ski powder is the holy grail of skiing. It can, however, be an elusive goal, and many give up after a few frustrating wrestling bouts with the formless white enemy. It need not be like this.

For a start you should never be intimidated by less than 20cm (8in) of snow (more if the snow is very light). Up to this depth, your body weight is still largely carried by the firm snow below the powder. No dazzling new technique is needed. Difficulties can arise because the smoothness and sound absorption of the powder dulls the feedback you expect from your skis. Moreover, the psychological effect of not being able to see your skis can be unnerving. The secret is to ski nor-

mally, tune in to the sensations in your feet, and stay strong – in other words don't let the powder pull your feet apart or trip you.

Once you get into deeper snow, the rules of the game change. You no longer have a firm surface under your skis, and the key is to become used to the feeling of floating on a cushion of powder. This, of course, takes time and experience.

Powder: the skier's nirvana.

EXERCISE

■ In order to develop a feel for your skis as they float beneath the surface, take every opportunity to get into powder. Cut into the powder at the side of a shallow piste, let your skis run straight and get used to the silent, springy ride. You don't need to sit back in order to prevent your tips from diving into the snow. Experiment with your stance until you are comfortable.

Experiment with your stance until you feel comfortable in powder.

Don't sit too far back.

A LA RECHERCHE DU SKI PERDU

Looking for a lost ski is one of the most frustrating ways to spend a great powder afternoon. Should you lose a ski, mark the point at which it released (frequently some distance above your body-crater). Then search systematically in an upside down fan shape below this point.

The surest way to avoid this problem is to use powder straps (powder leashes in the U.S.). If you are afraid of being hit by your ski, an alternative system uses brightly coloured ribbons. Tucked into your trouser cuffs, these should unroll if you fall, float to the surface and lead you to your lost ski.

If you lose a ski make sure you search systematically.

PLATFORM UNWEIGHTING IN POWDER

The easiest way to ski powder is to use platform unweighting. As you finish each turn, you allow pressure to build under your skis, forming a firm platform. From this base you can up-unweight and begin your next turn.

TIPS

■ Don't lean back. Keep your weight over your feet.

■ Distribute the pressure more evenly than usual between your skis: putting all your weight on the outside ski will make it sink. Also, keep your skis a little closer together.

■ Add power and smoothness by lifting your outside hand and pushing your feet forwards as you unweight.

■ Don't try to use your edges as you would on groomed snow: push instead against the entire soles of your feet. Push down through your heels at the end of the turn.

■ If you develop a comfortable rhythm, it should feel as though you are bouncing out of the snow at each turn.

1 As you finish each turn, anticipate the next by flexing down. Apply pressure through your heels to form a platform under your skis.

2 Plant your pole and extend to up-unweight.

3 Steer your skis into the fall line.

4 Continue to steer your skis, finishing the turn fully to regulate your speed.

COMPRESSION TURNS IN POWDER

A more elegant and less strenuous technique than platform unweighting is the compression turn (see page 161). This doesn't involve projecting the whole body out of the snow to initiate the turn: instead the skis are brought to the surface by retracting the legs. Skiing powder in this way is very similar to skiing big, rounded moguls: instead of letting the mogul compress your legs up under you, you let the build-up of pressure from the powder do this (hence the name). This is the most elegant way to ski powder and certainly the most sensuous.

1 Finish each turn by extending and pushing your heels into the snow to regulate your speed.

2 As the pressure builds under your heels, allow your legs to flex and bring your skis to the surface.

3 Steer your skis into the fall line.

4 Extend your legs, pushing your heels into the snow once again to regulate your speed.

CONDITIONS OFF PISTE

Unfortunately powder is not the only type of snow encountered off piste. Less pleasant varieties lurk.

HEAVY POWDER

All powder is not created equal. At higher temperatures, the moisture content of the fresh snow rises. The snowflakes stick together and pack densely. Instead of a fine spray being thrown up as you ski, large lumps are detached, and turning is hard work.

The best technique to adopt is platform unweighting (see page 178). Exaggerate the unweighting by punching with the outside hand and thrusting your feet forwards.

PORRIDGE

This is unfortunately not the smooth, creamy oats dish, but heavy, wet snow with lumps. It is either fresh snow that has fallen above freezing point or been rained on, or older melting rubbish. If not too deep, it can be skied in the same way as slush (see page 119). Otherwise, as with heavy powder, the only solution is to try platform unweighting. Porridge requires a lot of brute force and since it is the cause of many late afternoon accidents, it is sometimes known as leg-breaker snow.

Even heavy powder can lift your spirits.

Have fun in crud at higher speeds than you would normally contemplate.

CRUD

After a fall of powder, you will rarely be the only skier on the mountain. Ultimately, every powder slope ends up crisscrossed by tracks, and the resulting surface can be a difficult one to ski. One moment, your skis are slowed by the resistance of powder, the next, they shoot out into someone's old tracks. You try as long as possible to pretend that you are still skiing powder, but at some point you have to

Wind ridges, called sastrugi, are evidence of high winds and warn of avalanche danger.

admit it: you are skiing crud.

Look ahead and concentrate on the approaching terrain. Stay balanced over your skis, and stay strong: do not let the patches of powder catch your legs and pull you off balance. Try using more speed than you would normally on a packed slope of the same steepness. This will make your skis plane through the remaining powder, evening out the surface, and even if you fall it shouldn't hurt.

WINDBLOWN SNOW

Windblown or windpacked snow is the result of a snowfall accompanied by high winds. The wind action breaks up the flakes, allowing the snow to pack densely in a series of crusty ridges. Skiing windblown snow is rarely much fun and can be similar to skiing crust (see page 182).

Windblown snow also presents a strong avalanche danger, since slopes and cornices will be loaded and may release without warning.

SPRING OR CORN SNOW

At the end of the season, the snow goes through a daily cycle of melting under the action of the sun and refreezing at night. If you arrive at exactly the right time, when just the top inch or so has thawed, you will find a firm, consistent surface that can be a joy to ski. This is also a relatively safe time for roaming off piste.

The only trick to skiing spring snow lies in the timing: arrive too early and you will be skiing on an ice-rink; stay too long, and your skis will sink into a melting layer of slush. Try south-facing slopes earlier in the morning, saving the north-facing slopes for later, once they have thawed somewhat.

Porridge for breakfast.

Skiing Breakable Crust

Everyone who skis off piste will meet breakable crust at some point. It is what powder often turns into when the top level is repeatedly warmed and then refreezes. Like a crème brûlée, it consists of a hard crust on top of a soft under-layer. If the crust is very thin, you can ignore it and ski on the snow beneath. If it is very thick, you can stay on top of it, and may even enjoy some great skiing conditions (for spring snow, see page 181). But between these extremes lies one of the most difficult and dangerous of surfaces. It will support you until you try to turn, at which point you break through and fall.

THE SOFT TOUCH

The first thing to try when you encounter crusty conditions is to avoid breaking through. If you can stay on the surface, you are in control and less likely to trip.
- Ski as smoothly as possible.
- Try not to use your edges.
- Keep pressure evenly on both skis.
- Use up and down motion to absorb any shocks which might break through the surface.

THE JUMP TURN

Sometimes the crust will be too thin to bear your weight, yet too strong to allow you to ski normally, catching at your feet and tripping you. As its name suggests, a jump turn involves jumping your skis out of the snow, turning them in the air and landing with them in the new direction. It will usually get you out of trouble.

Jump turns (above) are very hard work. All but the most fanatic off-piste skiers head for the groomed slopes under these conditions.

If the crust is fragile, putting too much pressure on one ski may cause it to break through (below).

THE COMPRESSION TURN

If you persist in trying to ski off piste when the conditions are crusty, you had better perfect the compression turn.

1 Finish each compression turn by extending and pushing your heels into the snow.

2 Flex your legs to bring your skis out from under the crust. This is the tricky bit.

3 Steer your skis through the fall line.

4 Stay balanced as you finish the turn and your skis break through the crust once more.

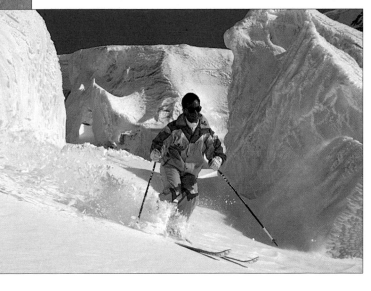

THE CHEAT

When all else fails, you can always cheat. Interspersing long traverses with kick turns is not very elegant, but is guaranteed to get you out of a nasty situation. Use a very shallow traverse to keep your speed down, and stop by performing a strong, slow swing to the hill (see page 125).

GULLIES AND EXTREME SLOPES

TESTING YOUR NERVE

Skiing the very steep, also called extreme skiing, can be a lot of fun. It is more than just a technical challenge. The element of fear tests your concentration and nerve to the utmost, as you savour the exhilaration of hanging weightless between turns. The sense of achievement lasts for years. Very steep slopes can be found in most large resorts, though they may be quite hard to reach. Certain ski areas, such as Chamonix in France, Blackcomb in British Columbia and Jackson Hole in the American Rockies, have become famous for their steep skiing.

For your first attempts, you should look for a very short, open slope, not a narrow gully. As you start to look further afield for steep skiing challenges, never forget that it is dangerous, and always take sensible precautions:
- Always go with someone who knows the slope.
- Never ski steep slopes under avalanche conditions (see pages 172-173).
- Never ski in big groups.
- Don't stand beneath other skiers.
- Don't be embarrassed to sidestep down if necessary.
- Don't ever take friends unless you are sure they can cope.

TIPS

- When you are airborne between turns, bend your knees to keep your tails from snagging on the slope behind you.
- On a really steep slope, you may have to jump off your uphill leg, as your downhill leg is already fully extended.
- If you fall and start to slide, use your poles to stop.

- If you start panicking, hold still for a while, breathe deeply and sidestep down (do not sideslip).
- If a companion gets panicky, try to calm them down. Persuade them to stand still, then start to sidestep down

Skiing the steep.

if it is safe to do so. Do not leave them alone unless you are sure they will stay where they are. On a purely selfish note, do not stand beneath them.

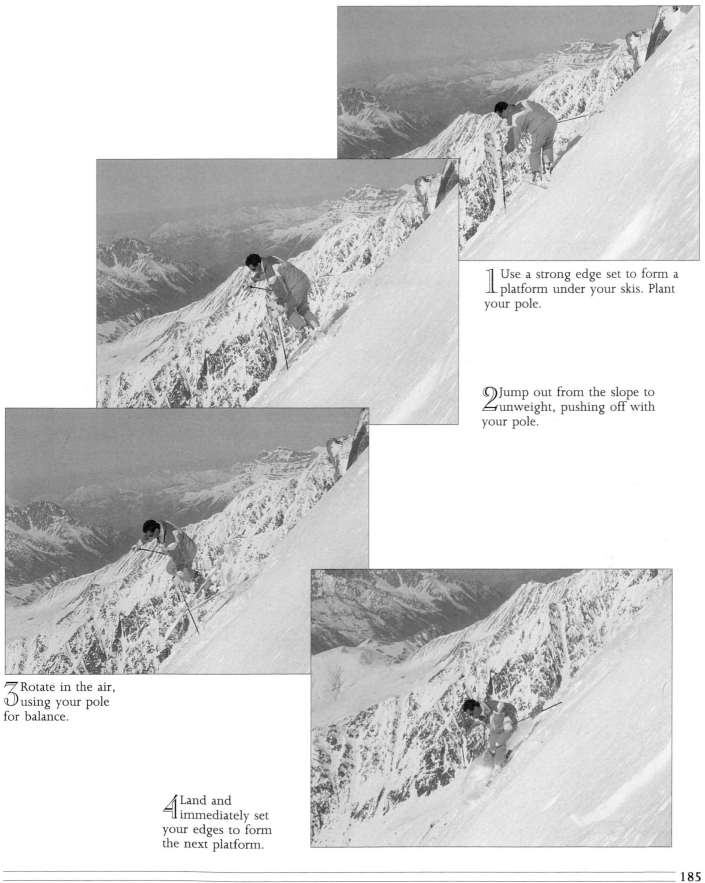

1 Use a strong edge set to form a platform under your skis. Plant your pole.

2 Jump out from the slope to unweight, pushing off with your pole.

3 Rotate in the air, using your pole for balance.

4 Land and immediately set your edges to form the next platform.

17 · COMPETITION

Over the years, the number of different skiing disciplines has snowballed,
starting with the nordic events, through alpine and then freestyle.
Each discipline now boasts a World Cup circuit, which takes competitors to a
different resort in the Alps, North America, Scandinavia or Japan each week
during the winter. This is backed up by the Europa Cup and Nor-Am
circuits, as well as FIS, national cup and local races.

ALPINE EVENTS

DOWNHILL, SLALOM, GIANT SLALOM AND SUPER-GIANT SLALOM

There are four alpine disciplines: downhill, slalom (or special slalom), giant slalom and super-giant slalom, all designed to test different types of skiing. The combined event is decided by one slalom and one downhill run.

Competitors are timed on a set course, which they are allowed to inspect, but not to ski, before their run. Starting last is normally a disadvantage, as courses become heavily rutted. In international competition, skiers are divided into seed groups, with the best ranked skiers skiing first; within the seed groups, start positions are decided at random.

Neil Munro (left) jumps a perfect kosak in competition.

DOWNHILL

The downhill is considered the ultimate test of nerve, the 'blue riband' event. The course consists of a single long run: in major championships, the winner's time should be around two minutes for men, and one minute 40 seconds for women. Gates are set only to keep speed within safe limits and to direct skiers away from obstacles.

The best downhiller is the one who can achieve the highest speed on the straight, hold the best line through the turns, and not be thrown off balance when covering 45m in the air at 115kph (70mph). Legendary courses include the Hahnenkamm in Kitzbühel and the Lauberhorn in Wengen for men, and the Kandahar in Garmisch for women. These offer a variety of terrains, testing the competitors over long, high-speed straights, sharp turns, hair-raising jumps and compressions.

Crash helmets are obligatory, and competitors use Lycra suits, curved ski poles, and long skis (around 2m23 for men and 2m15 for women) with flat tips, which offer maximum speed and stability and minimum air resistance.

Marc Girardelli in the World Cup at Val Gardena.

Vreni Schneider, dressed for slalom, wearing gauntlets, shin pads and helmet for protection. Note the tip deflectors, which may prevent a ski being hooked on the wrong side of the pole.

SLALOM

Slalom is one of two 'technical' disciplines (the other being giant slalom). It tests the skier in short-radius turns, requiring balance, agility and quick reactions. Alternate blue and red gates are set between 4 and 6 metres wide. The snow should be as hard as possible to slow the development of ruts. Competitors are timed over two runs on different courses, each usually taking around 50 seconds. Skis are typically 2m 05 for men, 1m 90 for women.

In order to ski the fastest line, competitors must commence their turns early, well above the gate. Starting turns late results in skidding and loss of speed. Rapid-gates, which fold when hit, allow skiers to take the pole across the shins or body without losing speed, and skiers adjust their path accordingly.

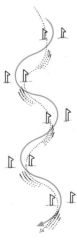

The ideal path through the gates
The fastest line down the course means turning early, well above the gate.

Alberto Tomba, the only skier ever to have successfully defended an Olympic gold medal in Alpine skiing, shows his form in the giant-slalom.

GIANT SLALOM

Giant slalom, or GS, is considered the ultimate technical challenge. It tests skiers in medium-radius turns and requires precision, an eye for the best line and feel for the skis. Skis are taken longer than for slalom, around 2m12 for men, 2m03 for women.

By driving hard out of each turn, competitors accelerate between gates and maximize speed. Gates are set wider than for slalom, and should be set on 'undulating and hilly terrain'. Once again there are two runs, each taking around 90 seconds, with the gates reset in between.

Competitors wear padding to protect themselves from the poles, and use aerodynamic suits.

SUPER-GIANT SLALOM

The super-giant slalom, or Super-G, was designed to be a meeting ground for technical skiers (slalom and GS specialists) and downhillers.

The single run takes around 90 seconds. The course is set to encourage a variety of medium- and long-radius turns at high speed. Two jumps can be included, one of which should require a change of direction.

Clothing is as for downhill, though slightly shorter skis are used.

FREESTYLE EVENTS

MOGULS, AERIALS AND BALLET

Freestyle has come a long way since it exploded onto the skiing world as hot-dogging in the early seventies. Back then skiers with names like The Silver Bullet, Boogie Mann and Wayne Wong rebelled against the straitjacket of alpine racing and gathered to compare tricks like the Franconia Super Dooper Wedeln and the Slow Dog Noodle. Lunacy, fun and illegal substances were the order of the day. The crowds were delighted, and by the mid-seventies a professional circuit with prize money of half a million dollars had grown up in the United States.

Disaster struck when two young skiers, lured by prizes of big money and cars, were crippled attempting double somersaults on unsafe jump sites. Sponsors began pulling out and the circuit collapsed. In 1979 the International Ski Federation (FIS) stepped in to ensure the survival and safety of the sport, renaming it freestyle (competitors now cringe when it is referred to as hot-dogging). Since then, the sport has gone from strength to strength, boasting its first World Cup in 1980, the inclusion of moguls as a full medal discipline at the 1992 Albertville Olympics in France, and of aerials at Lillehammer in Norway in 1994.

There are three freestyle disciplines: moguls, aerials and ballet; the combined event is decided on all three of these. Performances are scored according to tightly specified criteria by a panel of five or seven judges. As the sport has matured, these criteria have become ever more closely defined. This has resulted in consistency of judging, although sadly it has taken much of the 'free' out of freestyle.

Michael Liebreich in a moguls competition.

MOGULS

Moguls consists of 'one run of free skiing on a heavily moguled course', generally around 250m long, lasting 25 to 30 seconds. Skis are taken slightly shorter than for slalom, 1m90 to 2m for men, 1m80 to 1m90 for women. All skiers perform a single run, with the best eight or 16 contestants (depending on the size of the field) proceeding to the finals. Parallel knockout finals are difficult to judge and are becoming increasingly rare.

Fifty per cent of the skier's score is accounted for by the quality of skiing. Turns must be aggressive yet controlled. The upper body must be kept calm, and poles planted without unnecessary arm movements. Any falls, mistakes, losses of control and deviations from the fall line are heavily penalized.

Twenty-five per cent of the score is based on two jumps. These are marked on execution, height and technical difficulty. Commonly used jumps include spread eagles, twisters, daffies, kosaks and helicopters, as well as combinations of up to three of these.

The final twenty five per cent of the score is calculated from the skier's speed by comparison with a base time set before the competition.

AERIALS

Aerials is one of the most spectacular ski events for audiences. Skiers perform two different jumps off carefully prepared kickers, using short skis (around 1m70) and no poles. Scoring is made up of twenty per cent for air (the take-off, height and distance of the jump), fifty per cent for form (the skier's shape in the air, execution and precision of movement) and thirty per cent for a clean, safe landing.

Jumps are announced before take-off, and deviating from the announced jump results in a no-score.

The emphasis is on safety: jump sites are built to carefully controlled dimensions, with a long, steep landing area to reduce impact in case of a crash. Competitors practise their jumps into water during the summer months, and each new jump must be qualified by an international coach before it is allowed

By winning the silver in 1993, Richard Cobbing brought Britain its first World Championship medal in skiing since 1936.

to be performed on snow.

Many aerialists have backgrounds as gymnasts or trampolinists, though most are good skiers.

BALLET

The format of ski ballet is similar to that of figure skating. Skiers are marked on technical merit and artistic impression. The prepared course is a shallow slope of about 15 degrees, 150m long and 40m wide; competitors move down the slope as they perform their routine. They choreograph a series of pole flips, axels and linking steps 'blended together... into a well-balanced programme, performed in harmony with music of the skier's choice'.

Although ballet may seem far removed from the world of the ordinary skier, it requires a high degree of co-ordination and athleticism.

Jan Bucher of the USA executes a perfect pole flip.

NORDIC EVENTS

CROSS-COUNTRY, BIATHLON, JUMPING, COMBINED

Nordic competitions form skiing's strongest link with its past. Events include cross-country races at various distances, biathlon, ski-jumping and nordic combined.

CROSS-COUNTRY

In cross-country skiing, men compete over distances of between 10 and 50km, women between 5 and 30km. There are also relay events and mass races in which up to 20000 people start. Some of these can cover distances up to 150km. A course should be equally divided into thirds between uphill, downhill and more varied, undulating terrain. Cross-country skiing is one of the most physically demanding sports in the world.

In recent times, the sport has been split by the skating debate: races are now divided into classical, in which skating is not allowed, and freestyle, in which all techniques can be used.

The Engadine Marathon brings together thousands of skiers for a massed start.

BIATHLON

This discipline is a throwback to skiing's military past. It consists of a cross-country race, usually 20km with rifle shooting at four points, once after each lap. Competitors must control their breathing and hit five targets; penalties are imposed for missing. Three-skier relays and races over other distances also exist.

Toni Nieminen jumped to a place in the record books by winning two gold medals and a bronze at the 1992 Olympics at the age of 16.

SKI JUMPING

Jumping hills are divided into sizes between small (from 20m) to flying hills, which can be up to 185m high. Most major competitions use a 70- and a 90-metre hill. Competitors are awarded points for distance and style. Falls, wobbles or incorrect positions result in deduction of points and the best two of three jumps count.

Jumpers use very long (around 2m 40), flat skis. These have no edges and may have several grooves in the base to keep them straight in flight. Helmets are worn, and clothes tend to be slightly baggy to retain air and increase the distance of the jump.

The V-style position, flying with the skis' tails together and tips apart, first appeared in the early nineties and was rapidly adopted by most competitors. The extra distance more than made up for the loss of style points.

NORDIC COMBINED

This is a two-event competition consisting of a 15km cross-country race and a jump. The two best jumps of three from a 70m hill are counted, and competitors then set off cross country staggered in the order of their jump standings. There are also team events.

SPEED SKIING

THE FLYING KILOMETRE

Speed skiing, also known as the Flying Kilometre or the White Fear, consists of a straight tuck down a dizzyingly steep slope. The skier achieving the fastest speed across a designated timing area is the winner. The skill lies in maintaining the most aerodynamic position and allowing the skis to slide optimally.

Skis are long, around 2m40, with little or no side-cut. All equipment is appropriately aerodynamic.

At the Albertville Olympics, Michel Pruefer established a new world record with a speed of 229.29kph on the Les Arcs track.

HOW TO GET INTO COMPETITION

If you think that you might be the next Alberto Tomba, if you need extra motivation to work on your skiing, or if you simply want to have some fun, why not give competition a go?

OPEN COMPETITIONS

Many resorts offer the chance for interested skiers to have a go at racing. Some permanently have parallel courses set up, where you can pay to race against a friend. Others participate in nationally administered schemes, such as the American Nastar system: you ski a set course, comparing your time to a standard set by an international racer.

Open mogul or slalom competitions are sponsored by local businesses in many resorts. Visitors can enter, and prizes are given in various categories. The emphasis is usually on picnicking and having a good time.

If you start to become more serious, you can enter a pro-am competition, in which members of the public are invited to pit themselves against professional racers in parallel competitions. The moguls competitions are particularly popular, and prize money can be substantial.

SKI CLUBS AND NATIONAL SELECTION SYSTEMS

Almost every country has a system of ski clubs that organize training and competitions in each discipline.

In Britain, competitions are run on snow (in Scotland) and also on dry slopes. The Home Nations' (England, Scotland, Northern Ireland and Wales) Councils select racers for their national team from local clubs, and the British team is selected from these skiers by the British Ski Federation.

In the United States, the system is administered by the United States Ski Association, in Canada by the Canadian Ski Association.

Günther Mader celebrates his run at the Albertville Olympics in France, 1992.

18 · OTHER STYLES

Alpine skiing, on which this book has concentrated so far, has several close relatives. Not only is it fun to try another style, but in certain conditions it can even be preferable. The day the lifts are all closed because of high winds may be the day to rent the equipment and put in a few laps of cross-country skiing in a sheltered valley. Touring skis are ideal to widen your horizons and see some 'real' off-piste skiing. Monoskis and snowboards make light work of crust. Trying new techniques will broaden your perspective and may even improve your usual skiing.

This chapter does not aim to provide detailed instructions for alternative styles and sports, but tries to supply enough information for you to understand the basics, rent the equipment and enjoy an afternoon of something different.

Touring

Touring, also known as ski mountaineering, combines the technical pleasures of alpine with the freedom of cross-country skiing. By using special bindings and skins, the ski tourer is independent of the lift system and free to roam the mountains at will.

EQUIPMENT

Skis

These are similar to downhill skis, but slightly broader, softer and lighter. They have a hole at the tip so they can be pulled up a cliff by rope or used for a makeshift sledge or stretcher. They also usually have a notch at the tail to keep the skins in place. They are taken about 15cm shorter than your normal downhill skis for lightness and ease of turning in poor snow.

Haute Route towards Rosablanche.

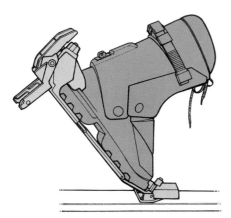

Touring ski binding (above)
Shovel, rucksack, boot, ski, skins, ski crampons,
transceiver, telescopic pole (right).

Bindings

Touring bindings have two settings: the heel is free during climbing, but fixed for skiing downhill. A wedge adds comfort when you are walking uphill. There are no brakes, so powder straps are necessary.

Boots

Normal alpine ski boots (especially rear entry) can be used, but special touring boots are advisable for longer tours. These have two settings, a raked-forward skiing position, and a free-flex setting for walking. The sole should be of non-slip material.

Poles

Telescopic poles that fold small if there is any tough climbing to be done, or convert to an avalanche search pole, can be used. However, normal poles with reasonable size baskets are fine for general touring.

Skins

Skins are used to walk up slopes, preventing the ski from sliding back downhill. At the top of a slope the skins are peeled off and carried in the rucksack for the descent. These days, they are made of mohair and polyester, rather than the traditional seal, and must be the right length for your skis. They are held on by a reusable adhesive, applied before a tour and left to dry overnight. It can be topped up with a spray if necessary.

To refold the skins after use, fold them adhesive to adhesive, bringing tip and tail to the centre. The sticky side must be kept dry. Do not roll skins and protect them against sun, heat and dirt.

Other equipment

For tours involving overnight stops in mountain refuges, the following items are recommended, though for shorter routes you may not need all of these:

■ Ski crampons: these fit between ski and boot and enable you to climb a steeper and icier slope than can be managed with skins alone.
■ Ice axe (with rubber spike protector).
■ Boot crampons.
■ Rope.
■ Avalanche transceiver (see page 175).
■ Avalanche shovel (to be carried by the last skier in the group).
■ Rucksack with waistband and side straps to hold skis when climbing.
■ Map, compass, altimeter.
■ Whistle. (The international distress sign is six calls per minute, with one minute silence.)
■ First-aid kit (see page 214).

■ Light flask and food.
■ Headlamp or torch for early starts and organizing your kit in the hut.

SAFETY

Part of the thrill of touring is the feeling of self-reliance and solitude offered by penetrating deep into the mountains. The negative side of this is that you are far from help in case of injury or accident. The advice given (see chapter 16, page 171) on safety off piste is of even greater importance to the tourer.

Estimate the length of your route and leave a safety margin, so you are not caught out as night falls. Leave early, before the snow has warmed up. Keep the group together. Don't be afraid to turn back or abandon your goal if conditions deteriorate. Respect the mountains.

Routes

Detailed walking maps have ski tours marked, but it is advisable to take a qualified guide. Some routes have become classics, such as the Haute Route between Chamonix, in France and Zermatt or Saas Fee, in Switzerland first done in 1903, which takes around a week.

4 Set off in the new direction.

Climbing

For climbing uphill, the heel of the binding is free. Climb with regular, rhythmic steps, and do not lift your skis off the snow. One skier leads, the others follow in the same track. The route should not be too steep uphill, but should follow a series of zigzags.

Uphill kick turn (below)

At the end of each rising traverse, an Uphill kick turn brings the skier round. Unlike in a normal kick turn (see pages 96-97), you face uphill, and turn only through about 150 degrees, until you are facing back in the new rising traverse.

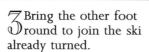

3 Bring the other foot round to join the ski already turned.

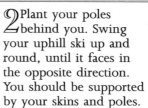

2 Plant your poles behind you. Swing your uphill ski up and round, until it faces in the opposite direction. You should be supported by your skins and poles.

1 Make sure your downhill ski is firmly placed.

UPHILL OFF PISTE

Securafix bindings slot into your normal downhill bindings. They enable you to walk uphill with a free heel and ski down using your own equipment.

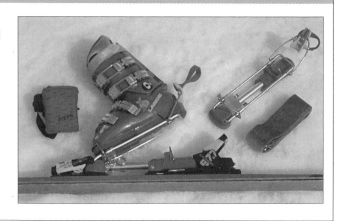

Descending

For skiing downhill, attach the heels of the bindings and adjust your boots if appropriate. Technique is identical to alpine skiing, except that a more conservative style should be adopted. Carrying a heavy pack, perhaps tired from walking uphill, and far from emergency services, this is not a good time to take chances.

Emergency stop

A dangerous slide can be arrested by using ski poles. Hold the two poles together, one hand by the handles, one hand down by the baskets, and dig the points into the snow or ice.

An emergency stop could save your life.

TOURS FOR TOURISTS

If you feel you would like to try touring, contact the guides' office in your resort. They should be able to put you into a group, select an appropriate route and provide guidance in hiring equipment.

CROSS-COUNTRY SKIING

This is one of the most popular forms of skiing, especially in Scandinavia. The equipment is light and you are not dependent on lifts. For overall fitness this style is the most beneficial, though it lacks the speed and excitement of alpine skiing.

EQUIPMENT

Skis

There is a wide variety of cross-country skis. They are very narrow (45-50mm) and generally have no edges. They are taken 20-30cm longer than your height. Test this by standing next to the ski and reaching up: the tip should come to your wrist. Racing skis are narrower than recreational skis, and are taken slightly shorter. True afficionados also distinguish between classical and freestyle (skating) skis.

Cross-country skis are very arched, so that when you are gliding, the camber pocket under your foot stands clear of the snow. Test this in the shop with a piece of paper: with your weight on both feet on a hard floor, you should be able to slide the paper under the skis; if you stand on one foot, the paper should be held firm.

Part of the base of the ski is either covered in scales or treated with a sticky wax to prevent it from sliding backwards. Scaled bases tend to be more stable, but they do not slide so well downhill. Beginners' skis and most rental skis are scaled, and for long promenades on variable snow this is the more convenient option.

The treatment of a waxed ski can be very complicated. Only the centre of the ski is treated and there are different waxes – hard, soft or klister - for

Traditional cross-country garb and scenery.

Cross-country equipment.

different temperatures and types of snow. If you use the wrong wax, you may end up with a lump of congealed snow stuck to the base or no grip at all.

Bindings, shoes and boots

The bindings are very light and hold only the tip of the toe, leaving the rest of the foot free. If you are skiing on prepared tracks, a shoe resembling a running shoe should be used. It must bend across the width while retaining its lateral rigidity. For skating, a slightly higher shoe exists, while for deeper snow you should use a boot.

There are several different standards for the bindings, but whichever binding you choose, make sure the boots and bindings are compatible.

Poles

These should be light but strong, and come up to the armpit. Racers take poles 5cm longer, skaters 15cm longer.

Clothes

Racers and very serious cross-country skiers wear 'spray-on' stretch suits. The traditional garb for recreational skiers is knickerbockers, thick woollen socks, a lumberjack shirt over a T-shirt or thermal vest, a zipped fleece and gaiters with spats. Gloves are important, but should be much thinner than alpine ones, with reinforced palms to protect against the rubbing of the pole. Sunglasses and a hat are also necessary.

TECHNIQUE

Many techniques are similar to those used in alpine skiing. The lack of edges, loose heels and absence of ankle support make cross-country skiing a bizarre sensation at first for alpine skiers, used to relying on their edges. This becomes painfully obvious in techniques such as the snowplough for which control of speed is crucial.

Walking with alternate step

The classic walk. Allow as long a glide as possible at the end of each step. The

The classic walk.

left arm thrusts forwards in time with the right leg.

Double pole plant

Use a strong double pole plant to propel yourself on the flat. To plant, reach forwards and keep your legs fairly straight.

Skating

In the 1980s skating came into its own, with special skis, boots and techniques enabling cross-country skiers to travel faster. It was controversial as it ruined carefully groomed tracks.

Double pole plant.

Climbing

Techniques such as herringbone climbing, uphill skating and in the steepest case, sidestepping, are similar to those used in alpine skiing.

Descending

The techniques for schuss, snowplough and parallel turns are similar to alpine skiing, though alpine skiers initially feel they are falling over backwards. Telemark turns can also be attempted (see pages 209-211).

TRACK ETIQUETTE

Several of the rules are the same as the FIS alpine code (see page 117). Other guidelines include:

Choice of tracks. On paths with more than one prepared track, skiers should choose the right-hand lane. Skiers in groups must keep on the right, behind each other.

Overtaking. A skier is not obliged to give way to an overtaking skier, but should allow a faster skier to pass whenever possible. A skier is permitted to overtake another skier on the left or right.

Encounter. Cross-country skiers who meet while skiing in opposite directions should keep to their right. A climbing skier should give way to a descending skier.

Poles. A cross-country skier should keep his poles close to his body whenever near another skier.

Control of speed. A cross-country skier should always adapt his speed to his personal ability, the prevailing terrain and visibility, and to the traffic on the course. Every skier should keep a safe distance from the skiers ahead. As a last resort, an intentional fall should be used to avoid collision.

Skating can be done double-sided...

...or on a single leg, keeping one ski in the track while the other does all the work.

Flex your body as you would for alpine skiing. Your knees should be over your feet.

Use a snowplough to slow yourself down.

Snowboarding

Snowboarding has become very popular in the last few years. In the mid-seventies, Californian surfers craving winter thrills began experimenting with 'snow-surf' boards. Within little more than a decade an established World Cup circuit had been set up, and snowboarding had graduated from fad status to become a major sport.

In some resorts every third person is on a board.

EQUIPMENT

Board

Snowboards are between 18-25cm wide at the waist, and between 1m and 1m 90 long. The edges, bases, side-cut and camber of a board are similar to those of a conventional ski.

Beginners should start on a 'freestyle' board, which has an upturned nose and tail, and an average to soft flex. For more advanced riders, boards vary just as skis do: a longer and stiffer board for speed, a shorter more flexible one for more varied terrain, a wider nose for powder. There are also specialist slalom boards, whose extreme side-cuts facilitate shorter, quicker turns. Freestyle boards are generally symmetrical with a softer flex to aid absorption of bumps, whereas racing boards are asymmetric.

Bindings and boots

The bindings are angled at between 55 and 35 degrees to the axis of the board for the front foot, and 10 to 45 degrees for the rear foot. Stance width varies between 40 and 60cm, depending on height, use and preference.

You must decide if you are *regular* (left foot in front) or *goofy* (right foot in front). There are several ways to discover this. Which foot do you put forwards if someone gives you an unexpected push from behind? Which foot do you put forwards to slide across a patch of ice?

There are two types of bindings. Soft bindings are pliable and comfortable. A plastic base with wrapover straps envelops the soft boot at the instep and toe. Freestylers prefer these as they offer greater flexibility of movement. Beginners should start on these, using ski boots or, preferably, proper soft boots. Hard or plate bindings offer more precise control but are less forgiving. Ski boots or special surf

boots, with a rigid shell but flexible ankle, are needed.

A security strap attaches the board to your ankle.

Other equipment

Clothing should be water- and windproof, and loose enough to allow freedom of movement. Knees need to be protected, especially for early attempts, and if the snow is hard a discreet foam layer over the coccyx is the better part of valour. Big, tough, padded gloves are necessary, since the hands are used for support.

TECHNIQUES

First moves

Snowboard technique is closer to skateboarding and surfing than skiing, but your knowledge of edge control, snow, unweighting and general balance and co-ordination will come in handy. If you can bear to miss a good day's alpine skiing, choose a day when there

Snowboarding equipment.

is a reasonable covering of new snow to cushion your early falls. A few lessons are recommended.

Start on a nursery slope: walk up and practise sideslipping. Try it both ways, toes facing downhill with the heel edge biting, then facing the slope with the toe edge biting, to get the feel of both positions. At this stage turn by sitting down.

Some teachers recommend you to use poles for the first day, since this avoids some of the tedium of falling around on your backside or knees, but your balance is affected, so it may not be worthwhile.

Basic stance

In the basic position you face down the slope, with seventy per cent of your weight on the front foot, legs bent, shoulders turned forwards, and arms out in front for balance.

Toeside slide turn (below)
Because of your asymmetrical stance on the board, you have to master two types of turn. Most snowboarders find the toeside turn (on the edge nearest to your toes) the easier to learn.

TIP

■ If you pick up too much speed, slide your rear foot out more abruptly while digging in the toes more.

Using the drag lifts
Release your back binding and fold it down so it doesn't drag in the snow.

Place the perch behind your front leg or under your rear arm. Trip the lift trigger as you pass if necessary. Either place the rear foot on the board between the front and rear binding, preferably on the 'stomp' pad, or use it to balance by running it in the snow alongside.

On chair lifts it is easier to position yourself to catch a chair with the rear foot free, but easier to disembark if both are attached. Swings and round-abouts.

1 Keep your arms in front for balance, with almost all your weight on your front foot.

2 Slide your rear foot to the outside of the turn, lifting your heels so the weight remains on the toeside edge.

3 Keep your upper body leaning towards the centre of the turn, into the hill.

Heelside slide turn (below)

You may find the heelside turn slightly harder to master than the toeside, but persevere and you'll get there in the end.

Linking turns

When you are ready to start linking your turns, remember the following points. Begin by straightening up at the end of each turn to flatten the board to the snow. Start sliding the rear foot in the opposite direction to the previous turn. Keep your arms in front for balance and correct weight transfer.

Development of technique

As you become more familiar with the board, keep your body in the fall line as much as possible, and use the side-cut of the board to aid your turns, until you can carve effectively.

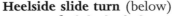

1 Starting in the basic stance, push on your heels, lifting your toes to flatten the board.

2 Keep your upper body turned towards the centre of the turn.

3 Slide your back foot towards the outside of the turn.

4 Remain on your heelside edge by bending your knees and pulling up your toes.

TIP

■ If you pick up too much speed, dig in your heel edge and slide the rear foot out more abruptly.

TELEMARK SKIING

For many years following the arrival of fixed-heel bindings, the telemark turn fell into disuse. It was rediscovered in the States in the late seventies and early eighties by skiers who were looking for new challenges.

For most skiers, the attraction of telemark skiing lies in the lightness of the equipment, the ease with which you can walk uphill for short distances and the grace of the turn. On gentle slopes or in shallow powder telemarking is elegant and attractive. Expert telemark skiers, however, are continually pushing the limits of performance of their equipment.

EQUIPMENT

Skis

Telemark skis are soft, with long tips. They are narrower and more waisted than alpine skis, but broader than cross-country skis. They may have edges for the whole length of the ski, or just for the part under the foot. Length should be decided with the wrist test (as for cross-country skis, see page 202) minus 5-10cm.

Bindings

Bindings hold only the front of the foot firmly, while leaving the heel free to rise. They generally use the 75mm three-pin Nordic Norm, but check that these are compatible with your boots. A safety strap attaches the ski to your leg in case of a release.

A classic telemark turn.

Boots

Telemark boots have a flexible sole so that the heel is free to move. A good boot should be supple longitudinally, but rigid laterally, not permitting the foot to twist to left or right. Boots have non-slip soles, and come up to the ankle or a little higher.

Poles

These are taken shorter than for cross-country skiing, since the position during skiing is lower. Try armpit length minus 5cm.

TECHNIQUE

Telemark stance

Practise gliding down a shallow slope with one foot in front of the other and your weight forwards. The tip of the rear ski should be almost level with the binding of the front ski.

Bend both knees to about 90 degrees. The body should remain in an almost vertical position.

Stand up again, and transfer smoothly to the other foot.

Telemark equipment.

The basic telemark position.

1 Plant your downhill pole.

Telemark turn

The telemark turn is a graceful, swooping curve, low on the inside knee, characteristic of this style of skiing.

2 Slide your uphill ski forwards, transferring your weight to it and start your turn

3 Steer your uphill ski through the fall line, balancing against the inner edge.

4 The inside ski trails and follows the outside ski.

5 Finish your turn.

Monoskiing

The monoski came into fashion in the early eighties, but lost favour with the arrival of the snowboard and its more natural stance and technique. It consists of a double-width alpine ski with two bindings mounted side by side. Monoskis have some attractions in powder, but generally do not track well on schusses and have poor grip on hard snow.

EQUIPMENT

Monoski
Monoskis are taken shorter than normal skis, generally between 1m 50 and 1m 85. A longer and broader ski should be used for powder, and a short, narrow ski for groomed snow.

Poles
These should be slightly longer than for alpine skiing, because a more upright stance is used.

TECHNIQUE

Putting on and taking off your ski
On a slope, insert your uphill foot first, so that you can set the ski's edge to avoid slipping downhill. When you take the ski off, release the downhill binding first.

Turns
In order to turn, use a more dynamic extension than in a two-skied turn, then thrust your hips and pelvis into the turn to steer. Use your arms and poles for balance; a double pole plant can be helpful.

The eighties produced yuppies, junk bonds and the monoski.

Traversing
Keep your weight on your uphill leg. Steer with your hips to keep the ski tracking correctly. The steeper the slope, the more you should turn your torso to face downhill, while keeping your edge rolled into the mountain.

Getting up
Use one hand uphill behind your hips, and push on the downhill pole at the same time.

Using the lifts
If you need to move on the flat or in the queue, release one foot and push yourself, as though pushing a scooter.

On chair lifts, try to get an outside seat. Once you are in position waiting to embark, you can replace your foot in its binding.

On drag lifts, keep both feet in the bindings, bending your knees out to the sides to put the perch between your legs. Keep your balance by making little jumps to re-establish equilibrium if necessary.

19 · HEALTH

BY DR J.B. LEVY, MA, MBBCHIR, MRCP

Since the mid-1970s the number of skiing accidents has decreased markedly,
mostly due to improvements in ski equipment.
On average a skier will have some sort of accident requiring medical
attention only every 200 days of skiing.

INJURIES

Most accidents on skiing holidays occur while actually on the slopes, though the number of non-skiing injuries is rising. Common causes include falls on icy roads, tobogganing and ice-skating accidents, and even collisions with airport luggage trolleys.

The nature of skiing injuries varies enormously. Fifty per cent are minor, such as muscular strains and bruises; the remainder include torn knee ligaments, leg fractures, dislocated thumbs and shoulders, and wrist injuries.

INJURY PREVENTION

The following precautions will help you to avoid injury on your holiday:
- Get fit before you leave (see chapter 2, page 20).
- Warm up before setting off each day (see page 61).
- Check your equipment, especially boots and bindings, regularly (see chapter 4, page 36).
- Follow the FIS safety code (see page 117).
- Keep an eye on other skiers.
- Stop when you become tired.
- Adjust your skiing to terrain and weather.
- Take care on the last run home. Everyone is as tired as you.
- Make sure your après-ski footwear is non-slip.

FIRST AID ON THE SLOPES

In any serious accident you should first ensure the safety of the injured skier, planting a pair of crossed skis above the accident site to warn others and mark the location. Then call the rescue service. One person should remain with the victim.

Keep the victim warm, remove skis but not boots, and do not give any alcohol. If there is any possibility of a spine or neck injury do not move them. Obvious bleeding should be staunched by direct pressure on the bleeding point and elevation if possible. Unconscious skiers should be carefully laid on their side, ensuring their mouth is empty of snow and vomit. If there is no palpable pulse or breathing, cardio-pulmonary resuscitation is needed.

Minor injuries on the slopes are much more common. Leg injuries, even if quite trivial, often entail a ride down in the rescue sledge (or blood wagon), as do most shoulder dislocations or broken arms. Arm injuries should be strapped with a scarf or jumper to minimize movement until medical advice can be sought, and legs splinted, using ski poles if necessary.

TREATMENT OF MINOR INJURIES

The treatment of most minor injuries (bruises, muscle, joint and minor ligament strains) involves four stages: rest, ice, compression and elevation (RICE). The affected limb should be fully rested for 24 hours. Apply ice to the injury within 30 minutes to minimize swelling, keeping it in place until the skin turns pink. Compression with a tight (elasticated) bandage, and elevation of the affected limb for from 2 to 24 hours will also help to avoid swelling.

This treatment will reduce inflammation and should allow you to resume skiing as soon as possible. Start gently and make sure that you ade-

quately support the injury. If pain or swelling persist, consult a local doctor, who will probably suggest a common anti-inflammatory medication.

Particular care must be taken over knees; if rapid swelling occurs after even a trivial injury, you may have damaged a ligament and need urgent medical attention. Once a knee has been damaged it tends to be less stable, and many skiers subsequently find a knee brace helpful. These range from simple neoprene bandages to major works of engineering with titanium struts and hinges. If you are worried, or have had a serious joint injury, speak to your doctor.

INSURANCE

- Before putting on your skis, you must be adequately insured. Cover should include illness and accidents, both on and off the ski slopes. It should include rescue from the mountain, treatment, hospitalization and repatriation.
- If you will be skiing off piste, check that your insurance covers this, as many policies exclude rescue outside marked ski areas. You should also insure against personal accident (loss of earnings, death, disability) and personal liability. You may also want to insure your ski equipment against loss or theft.
- Note that most general travel insurance excludes winter sports, and most winter sports insurance excludes competition.

COLD, ALTITUDE AND ULTRAVIOLET

HYPOTHERMIA

Hypothermia occurs when your body temperature, normally 37°C (98.6°F), falls beneath 35°C (95°F). At this level the function of various cells and organs is impaired. This is potentially fatal. You are more likely to suffer hypothermia when exposed to the wind, as your body loses heat much more rapidly. Hypothermia can best be prevented by wearing appropriate clothes: they must have sufficient insulation, as well as wind- and waterproof outer layers; a hat is also important (see page 49). Children must be especially well dressed.

It is particularly important to notice signs of hypothermia in your companions, as it is difficult to diagnose in yourself. First a person feels cold, but often doesn't complain. Then you may notice a change in behaviour; they become irritable, aggressive, confused and later drowsy. It is vital to be aware of these signs, particularly when you are touring or skiing off piste.

If you suspect someone in your group has hypothermia, stop at once. Make sure you are in a safe spot, and that the person is fully dressed and protected from snow and wind. If you can reach a hut or restaurant, warm the person with hot drinks. Under no circumstances should someone with hypothermia be given alcohol, as the increased bloodflow to the extremities can lead to a further dangerous drop in core temperature. Cigarettes may result in the victim developing frostbite due to reduced bloodflow to the extremities. If you cannot get to shelter, huddling together should warm the affected person, but this takes time.

FROSTBITE AND FROSTNIP

Frostbite or frostnip occur when your extremities (fingers, toes, ears, nose and cheeks) become so chilled that their temperature drops below freezing point. If this is caught quickly, it is fully reversible (frostnip); if not, the result may be the loss of tissue (frostbite). Less extreme forms of cold injury include chapped lips and skin.

The first symptoms are an uncomfortable coldness that then becomes painful and finally numb. At the onset of frostnip, the affected area looks pale or even white, and it can easily be spotted on a companion's nose, cheeks or ears. Later the patch turns purplish, before becoming hard and frozen. Occasionally it manifests by blistering.

As with hypothermia, frostbite can be prevented by wearing good clothing, protecting extremities, and watching your companions. As soon as you notice any symptoms, stop in a safe place and rewarm the affected area. Continuing to ski exacerbates the damage. Hands and feet should be put inside jumpers or trousers, close to warm skin, and faces wrapped in warm scarves. Do not rub the affected area, as the skin will be fragile and liable to tear. If the frostbite is well established (frozen-feeling tissue with no recovery on rewarming) you should go straight to hospital, where doctors will try to minimize the damage. Once again, alcohol or cigarettes will only make matters worse.

HIGH ALTITUDE

Altitude causes a problem only if you ski for extended periods at altitudes above 3000m (about 10000ft). At this height the amount of oxygen available is reduced and you may start to feel particularly tired after minimal exertion. You may also feel weak or suffer from headaches, particularly during the first few days. Wait a few days to acclimatize before going to the highest point in your resort.

Skiers who stay at these altitudes for longer periods or ascend too rapidly may develop acute mountain sickness (AMS). This starts with tiredness, headaches, nausea and dizziness, but can rapidly progress, through changes in personality and behaviour, to a life threatening condition. If you suspect someone in your group has acute mountain sickness, you must descend immediately, as this is the only way of reversing the condition.

THE SUN

At altitude, the effect of the sun on your skin and eyes can be highly dangerous. Always use effective protection (see page 49).

FIRST AID KIT

- Regular medication.
- Painkillers, e.g. Paracetamol.
- Motion-sickness tablets.
- Anti-inflammatories, e.g. Ibuprofen, Advil.
- Sticking plasters.
- Elasticated bandage.
- Sun cream.
- Contraceptives.
- Blister protection, e.g. Second Skin/Compeed.

OTHER HEALTH FACTORS

If you suffer from a chronic condition such as epilepsy, diabetes or heart disease, or are pregnant, discuss skiing plans with your doctor before going.

The following are general guidelines; your own doctor should be able to provide more information.

PREGNANCY

There are two things the pregnant skier should consider - the effect of skiing on the foetus, either through falling, vigorous exercise or tiredness, and the effect of the foetus on you. Both depend on the stage of pregnancy and your individual experience.

From about the seventh month, skiing is physically difficult. In late pregnancy it is also potentially dangerous as it could induce premature labour. The best time is from 12 to 28 weeks. Try not to fall heavily; avoid high speeds, crowded pistes and high altitudes.

Women who have had previous miscarriages should not ski. Pregnant women are at increased risk of leg vein thrombosis during prolonged periods of immobility, so make sure you move your legs and feet while in the aeroplane or car, and keep well hydrated.

DIABETES

Skiing can be fully enjoyed by diabetics, providing you take the appropriate precautions. Do not ski alone, and let your companions know that you are diabetic: warn them to give you sugar if you develop symptoms of hypoglycaemia. The risk of hypothermia is higher if you develop hypoglycaemia: the sensation of severe cold and the ability to shiver are both lost.

Karen Liebreich, seven months pregnant, skiing very carefully.

Skiing is a high energy activity, using about 10kCal/minute. You must therefore increase your caloric intake. As a rough guide you should eat an extra bar of chocolate in the morning (at the top of the first lift is the best time), have about 100kCal extra for lunch, and a mid-afternoon snack. And carry glucose or sweets with you.

A medicalert bracelet may be lifesaving in emergencies, and some form of official identification will avoid problems with needles at customs. The British Diabetic Association or American Diabetes Association are good sources of information.

EPILEPSY

As with any sport, a balance must be established between restricting activities and exposing yourself (or your family or friends) to danger. Frequent fits unfortunately preclude skiing, but well controlled epileptics may ski. They should do so in company and not in extreme situations.

ASTHMA

Cold weather makes asthma worse, so it is vital to continue taking your regular medication. Ventolin (salbutamol) or similar bronchodilator inhalers (e.g. Bricanyl, terbutaline) should be used before you go out into the cold, and should be carried on the slopes.

THE OLD MAN AND THE SKI

There is no upper age limit for skiing. As long as you remain fit and agile, and have mastered a good basic technique, there is no reason why you should not take advantage of cheap lift passes offered to pensioners by most resorts.

SKIING FOR PEOPLE WITH DISABILITIES

Skiing is an excellent sport for those with physical or mental disabilities, such as multiple sclerosis, cerebral palsy, hemiplegia, spinal-cord injuries, spina bifida, muscular dystrophy, amputation, blindness and deafness. It offers a sense of freedom and independence, exhilaration and the opportunity to share holidays and experiences with non-disabled friends.

Specialized equipment, such as outrigger skis, flip-skis, canting wedges or sit-skis are available to make the sport accessible. Certain resorts, such as St Johann in Tirol, Winter Park in Colorado and Anzère in Switzerland are particularly appropriate because of their layout and access to the slopes.

In Britain, the Uphill Ski Club and the British Ski Club for the Disabled organize lessons and training sessions for people with disabilities and for their guides at dry ski slopes, as well as holidays in the Alps. The charity Back-Up reintroduces spinally injured sportspeople to active sports. (See page 227 for addresses.)

Champion sit-skier Matthew Stockford in a slalom competition.

20 · SKI RESORTS

This chapter lists a selection of ski resorts throughout the world (see also chapter 3, Choosing a Holiday). It is intended to give you an idea of the size of resorts and the type of skiing available, however, it should only be used as a rough guide. Travel agents and national tourist offices can provide more specific and up-to-date information, or you can consult detailed annual guide books.

Resort	Altitude (m/ft) Highest lift	No. of lifts*	beg	int	adv	non	Linked areas
ANDORRA							
Arinsal	1550/5085 2500/8202	15	■	■			
Pal	1780/5840 2358/7736	14	■	■			
Pas de la Casa	2050/6725 2600/8530	9	■	■			
Soldeu/Tarter	1800/5905 2560/8399	22	■	■			
AUSTRALIA							
Charlotte Pass, NSW	1821/5974 2000/6560	5	■				
Falls Creek, Vic	1580/5183 1777/5830	22		■			
Mt Baw Baw, Vic	1480/4855 1563/5128	8	■	■			
Mt Buffalo, Vic	1400/4593 1610/5282	7	■				
Mt Buller, Vic	1600/5250 1788/5866	24	■	■			
Mt Hotham, Vic	1750/5740 1846/6056	8	■	■			
Perisher-Smiggins, NSW	1718/5636 2054/6739	30	■	■			
Thredbo, NSW	1370/4495 2037/6683	15	■	■			
AUSTRIA							
Alpbach	1015/3330 2025/6643	21	■	■			
Altenmarkt	856/2808 1700/5577	9	■	■		■	
Auffach	870/2854 1770/5807	12	■				
Badgastein	1080/3543 2686/8812	23(51)			■	■	Gastein Superski
Bad Hofgastein	900/2952 2670/8760	17(51)			■	■	Gastein Superski
Ellmau	820/2690 1530/5019	11(102)	■	■			Kaiser Brixental/ St Johann in Tirol
Fieberbrunn	795/2608 1650/5413	15(23)	■				
Finkenberg	825/2706 2075/6807	7(151)	■	■			Zillertal Superski
Fulpmes	937/3074 2260/7414	12(30)	■	■			
Galtür	1600/5250 2625/8612	12(30)	■	■			Silvretta
Gargellen	1430/4691 2300/7546	9	■				Montafon
Gerlos	1250/4100 2290/7513	32	■	■			
Hinterglemm	1100/3609 2096/6876	23(60)	■	■	■		Saalbach Hinterglemm
Hinterstoder	600/1969 1900/6234	17	■				
Hintertux	1500/4920 3265/10712	19(151)	■	■			Zillertal Superski
Hochsölden	2105/6906 3050/10006	9(33)	■	■	■		Sölden
Hopfgarten	622/2040 1825/5987	10(91)	■	■			Kaiser Brixental
Igls	870/2854 2247/7372	6(34)	■	■			Innsbruck
Innsbruck	574/1883 2260/7414	4(34)	■	■			
Ischgl	1400/4593 2864/9396	35(60)		■		■	Silvretta
Kaprun	864/2834 3392/11128	15(55)	■	■			Europa Sport Ski Region
Kirchberg	850/2788 1920/6299	15(64)	■	■			Kitzbühel
Kitzbühel	800/2624 2000/6560	64	■	■	■		
Kuhtai	2020/6627 2490/8169	10	■	■			
Lech	1450/4757 2450/8038	21(87)	■	■	■		Arlberg
Leogang	800/2624 1914/6280	12(60)	■	■			Saalbach Hinterglemm
Lermoos	1004/3294 2070/6791	8	■				
Mallnitz	1200/3937 2650/8694	11	■				
Mayrhofen	640/2100 2278/7473	18(151)	■	■		■	Zillertal Superski
Mutters	830/2723 1799/5902	6(34)	■				Innsbruck
Neustift	993/3258 2080/6824	8	■	■			
Niederau	825/2706 1900/6234	11(37)	■	■			Wildschonau

Key: beg = beginner, int = intermediate skier, adv = advanced skier, non = non-skier.
*Figures in brackets indicate approximate total number of lifts in adjoining valleys or within the same area for which a combined ski pass can be purchased.

| | Altitude (m/ft) | | No. | Recommended for: | | | | |
	Resort	Highest lift	of lifts*	beg	int	adv	non	Linked areas
Obergurgl	1930/6332	3082/10111	13(23)	■	■			Hochgurgl/Untergurgl
Obertauern	1740/5708	2313/7588	27	■	■			
Saalbach	1010/3313	2096/6876	19(60)	■	■			Saalbach Hinterglemm
St Anton	1304/4278	2800/9186	30(87)		■	■		Arlberg
St Christoph	1800/5905	2165/7103	19(87)	■	■			Arlberg
St Johann (in Pongau)	800/2624	1100/3609	12(120)	■				3-TalerSchischaukelland
St Johann (in Tirol)	650/2132	1700/5577	18(15)	■	■			Fieberbrunn
Scheffau	752/2467	1678/5505	9(91)	■	■			Kaiser Brixental
Schladming	735/2411	2015/6611	29(75)	■	■			Ski Paradies
Schruns	700/2296	2380/7808	13	■	■		■	
Seefeld	1200/3937	2075/6807	20	■	■		■	
Serfaus	1427/4682	2700/8858	17	■	■			
Sölden	1370/4495	3200/10498	24(33)	■	■	■		Hochsölden
Söll	795/2608	1830/6004	12(91)	■	■			Kaiser Brixental
Steinach	1050/3445	2200/7218	7	■				
Stuben	1410/4626	2412/7913	5(87)	■	■			Arlberg
Wagrain	900/2952	2015/6611	15(120)		■			3-TalerSchischaukelland
Waidring	781/2562	1860/6102	16	■	■			
Westendorf	790/2592	1800/5905	13(91)	■				Kaiser Brixental
Zell-am-See	750/2460	1965/6447	29(55)	■	■		■	Europa Sport Ski Region
Zell-am-Ziller	580/1903	2408/7900	21	■				
Zürs	1720/5643	2811/9222	10(87)	■	■			Arlberg
BULGARIA								
Borovets	1323/4340	2560/8399	13	■	■			
Pamporovo	1620/5315	1937/6355	16	■	■			
Vitosha	1800/5905	2295/7530	10	■				
CANADA								
Blackcomb, BC	675/2214	2284/7493	13(27)		■	■		Whistler
Lake Louise, Al	1544/5065	2385/7825	10	■	■	■		
Mt Sainte Anne, Qu	175/574	800/2624	12		■			
Mt Saint-Sauveur, Qu	203/666	416/1365	10		■			
Mt Tremblant, Qu	265/869	914/2998	11	■	■			
Mount Norquay, Al	1630/5348	2134/7001	5	■	■			
Nakiska, Al	1535/5036	2260/7414	5		■			
Sunshine Village, Al	1658/5439	2729/8953	12		■			
Whistler, BC	675/2214	2260/7414	33(13)	■	■	■		Blackcomb
FRANCE								
Alpe d'Huez	1859/6099	3320/10892	87	■	■			Grandes Rousses
Les Arcs	1600/5250	3226/10584	79	■	■	■		
Argentière	1250/4100	3290/10793	9(209)		■	■		Mont Blanc
Avoriaz	1800/5905	2300/7546	40(162)	■	■	■		Portes du Soleil
Barèges (Pyrenees)	1250/4100	2340/7677	26(56)	■	■			La Mongie
Briançon	1340/4396	2685/8809	11(77)	■	■			Grand Serre-Chevalier
Les Carroz	1140/3740	2480/8136	17(81)	■	■			Grand Massif
Cauterets-Lys	1000/3280	2350/7710	18	■	■			
Chamonix	1070/3510	3842/12605	48(209)		■	■	■	Mont Blanc

Key: beg = beginner, int = intermediate skier, adv = advanced skier, non = non-skier.
*Figures in brackets indicate approximate total number of lifts in adjoining valleys or within the same area for which a combined ski pass can be purchased.

Resort	Altitude (m/ft) Resort	Highest lift	No. of lifts*	beg	int	adv	non	Linked areas
Champagny	1250/4100	3250/10663	7(111)	■	■			Grande Plagne
Chamrousse	1650/5413	2225/7300	26	■	■			
Chapelle d'Abondance	1000/3280	1800/5905	12(162)	■				Portes du Soleil
Châtel	1200/3937	2300/7546	50(162)		■			Portes du Soleil
La Clusaz	1100/3609	2590/8497	56	■	■			
Les Coches	1450/4757	2685/8809	5(111)	■				Grande Plagne
Combloux	900/2952	2600/8530	21(209)	■	■			Mont Blanc
Les Contamines	1164/3819	2480/8136	25	■	■			
Courchevel	1300-1850/ 4265-6070	3200/10498	67(220)	■	■	■		Trois Vallées
Les Deux Alpes	1650/5413	3568/11706	63	■	■			
Flaine	1600/5250	2500/8202	31(81)	■	■			Grand Massif
Les Gets	1160/3806	2440/8005	32(162)	■	■			Portes du Soleil
Le Grand-Bonand	1000/3280	2100/6890	40	■	■			
Les Houches	1010/3313	1900/6234	15(209)	■	■			Mont Blanc
Isola 2000	2000/6560	2625/8612	23	■	■			
Les Karellis	1600/5250	2500/8202	18	■	■			
Megève	1100/3609	2350/7710	43(209)	■	■		■	Mont Blanc
Les Menuires	1855/6086	2850/9350	54(220)	■	■	■		Trois Vallées
Méribel	1400/4593	2910/9547	49(220)	■	■	■		Trois Vallées
La Mongie (Pyrenees)	1800/5905	2500/8202	30(56)	■	■			Barèges
Montchavin	1250/4100	3265/10712	15(111)	■	■			Grande Plagne
Montgenèvre	1850/6070	2701/8861	23(100)	■	■			Milky Way
Morzine	1000/3280	2440/8005	29(162)	■	■			Portes du Soleil
La Norma	1345/4412	2750/9022	18	■				
Orcières-Merlette	1850/6070	2655/8710	29	■	■			
Peisey-Vallandrey	1300/4265	2400/7874	15(79)	■	■			Les Arcs
La Plagne	1800/5905	3250/10663	33(111)	■	■		■	Grande Plagne
Pra-Loup	1600/5250	2500/8202	55	■	■			
Risoul	1850/6070	2750/9022	18(54)	■	■			La Forêt Blanche
La Rosière	1830/6004	2400/7874	18(52)	■	■			La Thuile
Les Rousses	1100/3609	1680/5512	39	■	■			
Les Saisies	1600/5250	1950/6397	24	■	■			
St François-Longchamp	1400/4593	2550/8366	14(47)	■	■			Le Grand Domaine
St Gervais	850/2788	2500/8202	26(209)	■	■			Mont Blanc
Samoëns	720/2362	2480/8136	17(81)	■	■			Grand Massif
Le Sauze	1400/4593	2440/8005	24	■	■			
Les Sept Laux	1350/4429	2400/7874	35	■	■			
Serre-Chevalier	1400/4593	2830/9285	75(77)	■	■			Grand Serre-Chevalier
Superdevoluy	1455/4773	2510/8235	32	■	■			
Super Lioran	1160/3806	1850/6070	24	■	■			
Tignes	2100/6890	3656/11995	98(206)	■	■	■		Espace Killy
La Toussuire	1450/4757	2400/7874	18(41)	■	■			Le Grand Large
Valberg	1650/5413	2025/6644	21	■	■			
Val Cenis	1400/4593	2800/9186	23	■	■			
Val d'Allos	1800/5905	2600/8530	22	■	■			
Val d'Isère	1850/6070	3260/10695	98(206)		■	■		Espace Killy
Valfréjus	1500/4920	2730/8956	13	■	■			
Valloire	1430/4691	2600/8530	25(35)	■	■			Le Crey du Quart
Valmeinier	1500/4920	2575/8448	33	■	■			
Valmorel	1400/4593	2550/8366	29(47)	■	■			Le Grand Domaine
Val Thorens	2290/7513	3399/11152	37(220)	■	■	■		Trois Vallées
Vars	1650/5413	2750/9022	33(54)	■	■			La Forêt Blanche
Villard de Lans	1130/3707	2015/6611	37	■	■			

Key: beg = beginner, int = intermediate skier, adv = advanced skier, non = non-skier.
*Figures in brackets indicate approximate total number of lifts in adjoining valleys or within the same area for which a combined ski pass can be purchased.

| | Altitude (m/ft) | | No. | Recommended for: | | | | |
	Resort	Highest lift	of lifts*	beg	int	adv	non	Linked areas
GEORGIA								
Gudauri	2158/7080	3326/10912			■			
GERMANY								
Bayerischzell	801/2630	2000/6562	26	■	■			
Berchtesgadener Land	560/1837	1800/5905	33	■	■			
Garmisch-Partenkirchen	708/2323	2964/9724	54	■	■			
Oberstaufen	856/2808	1700/5577	35	■	■			
ITALY								
Abetone	1388/4554	1982/6502	27	■	■			
Aprica	1180/3871	2575/8448	30	■	■			
Arabba	1615/5298	2960/9711	26(470)	■	■	■		Superski Dolomiti
Bardonecchia	1312/4304	2715/8907	27	■	■			
Bormio	1217/3993	3020/9908	27(60)	■	■		■	Superpool
Campitello	1440/4724	2952/9684	7(470)	■	■			Superski Dolomiti
Canazei	1465/4806	2930/9613	9(470)	■	■			Superski Dolomiti
Cavalese	1000/3280	2300/7546	36	■	■			
Cervinia	2144/7034	3680/12073	37(73)	■	■			Zermatt
Clavière	1750/5740	2290/7513	11(100)	■	■			Milky Way
Cortina d'Ampezzo	1280/4199	3213/10543	52	■	■	■		
Corvara	1568/5144	2557/8389	15(470)	■	■			Superski Dolomiti
Courmayeur	1224/4016	3520/11548	25		■		■	
Folgarida-Marilleva	1300/4265	2179/7149	23	■	■			
Gressoney	1699/5574	2736/8976	21	■	■			
Limone	1010/3313	2075/6807	33	■	■			
Livigno	1816/5958	2800/9186	28(60)	■	■			Superpool
Macugnaga	1362/4468	2900/9514	13	■	■			
Madesimo	1555/5102	2929/9609	23	■	■			
Madonna di Campiglio	1520/4987	2590/8497	32	■	■	■		
Montecampione	1200/3937	1800/5905	17	■	■			
Nevegal	1030/3379	1668/5471	14	■				
Ortisei	1236/4055	2518/8261	6(470)	■	■			Superski Dolomiti
Passo Tonale	1883/6178	3106/9895	41	■	■			
Piancavallo	1300/4264	2000/6562	18	■	■			
Pila	1790/5873	2620/8596	13	■	■			
La Polsa	1219/4000	1707/5600	12	■				
Ravascletto	975/3200	1707/5600	12	■	■			
San Martino	1465/4806	2685/8809	28	■	■			
Sansicario	1700/5577	2820/9252	12(100)	■	■	■		Milky Way
Santa Caterina	1737/5699	2498/8195	14(60)	■				Superpool
San Vigilio	1201/3940	2275/7464	33(134)	■				Valdaora, Riscone
Sauze d'Oulx	1568/5144	2820/9252	28(100)	■	■			Milky Way
Selva di Val Gardena	1567/5141	2518/8261	85(470)	■	■	■	■	Superski Dolomiti
Sesto	1310/4298	2200/7218	31	■	■			
Sestriere	2035/6676	2820/9252	26(100)	■	■			Milky Way
Terminillo	1614/5295	2212/7259	13	■	■			
La Thuile	1441/4727	2642/8668	34(52)	■	■			La Rosière
Valtournenche	1528/5013	3085/10121	10	■	■			
Vigo/Pozza di Fassa	1382/4534	2135/7004	13	■				

Key: beg = beginner, int = intermediate skier, adv = advanced skier, non = non-skier.
*Figures in brackets indicate approximate total number of lifts in adjoining valleys or within the same area for which a combined ski pass can be purchased.

| | Altitude (m/ft) | | No. | Recommended for: | | | | |
	Resort	Highest lift	of lifts*	beg	int	adv	non	Linked areas
JAPAN								
Appi Kogen	505/1657	1328/4357	30	■	■			
Daisen	740/2428	1140/3740	23	■	■	■		
Furano	235/771	1209/3966	16	■	■	■		
Happo One	750/2460	1820/5971	35		■			
Inawashiro	700/2296	1350/4429	14	■	■			
Ishiuchi Maruyama	256/840	920/3018	36	■	■			
Naeba	900/2953	1789/5869	39		■	■		
Niseko	400/1312	1309/4294	20		■	■		
Nozawa Onsen	560/1837	1650/5413	40	■	■			
Shiga Kogen	1410/4626	2305/7562	79	■	■	■		
Shizukuishi	426/1397	1356/4449	16		■			
Sugadaira Kogen	1271/4170	2207/7241	30	■				
Tazawako	500/1640	1200/3937	18	■	■			
Tugaike Kogen	800/2625	1700/5577	30	■				
Zao	850/2788	1600/5249	42	■	■			
KASHMIR								
Gulmarg	2730/8596	4138/13576	5	■	■			
LIECHTENSTEIN								
Malbun	1605/5266	2006/6581	7	■	■			
NEW ZEALAND								
Cardrona	1463/4800	1829/6000	5	■	■			
Coronet Peak	1518/4980	1650/5413	7		■		■	
Mt Cook National Park	–	–	heliskiing		■	■		
Mt Hutt	1300/4265	2047/6716	10	■	■	■		
Porter Heights	1280/4199	1981/6499	5	■	■			
Rainbow	1450/4757	1800/5905	4	■	■			
Remarkables	1600/5250	1900/6234	5	■	■			
Treble Cone	1413/4636	2073/6801	4	■	■			
Turoa	1600/5250	2320/7611	10	■	■			
Waioru Nordic	nordic, telemark skiing							
Whakapapa	1385/4544	200/6560	22		■	■		
NORWAY								
Geilo	800/2624	1060/3478	18	■	■			
Hemsedal	650/2132	1430/4691	14	■	■			
Lillehammer/Hafjell	180/590	1050/3445	8	■	■	■		
Oppdal	545/1788	1280/4199	15	■	■			
Trysil	550/1804	1000/3280	20	■	■			
Voss	100/328	945/3100	10	■	■			

Key: beg = beginner, int = intermediate skier, adv = advanced skier, non = non-skier.
*Figures in brackets indicate approximate total number of lifts in adjoining valleys or within the same area for which a combined ski pass can be purchased.

| | Altitude (m/ft) | | No. | Recommended for: | | | | Linked areas |
	Resort	Highest lift	of lifts*	beg	int	adv	non	
POLAND								
Zakopane	740/2428	1985/6512	5	■	■			
ROMANIA								
Poiana Brasov	1060/3478	1770/5807	13	■	■			
Sinaia	800/2624	1999/6560	13	■				
SCOTLAND								
Aviemore/Cairngorm	550/1804	1100/3609	17	■	■			
Glencoe	639/2096	1100/3609	6	■	■			
Glenshee	611/2004	919/3015	26	■	■			
The Lecht	609/2000	702/2600	10	■	■			
SLOVENIA								
Bled	501/1644	1271/4171	19	■	■			
Kranjska Gora	810/2657	1640/5380	18	■	■			
SPAIN								
Alto Campo	1700/5577	2149/7050	11	■	■			
Astun	1650/5413	2324/7624	10	■	■			
Baqueira-Beret	1500/4920	2510/8235	22	■	■			
Boí-Taüll	2038/6686	2457/8061	7	■				
Candanchu	1450/4757	2400/7874	22	■	■			
Cerler	1505/4937	2364/7756	12	■	■			
El Formigal	1500/4920	2350/7710	19	■	■			
Llessuí	1445/4741	2430/7972	6	■				
Lunada	1300/4265	1590/5216	7	■				
Masella	1600/5250	2530/8300	11	■	■			
La Molina	1590/5216	2534/8315	20	■	■			
Panticosa	1200/3937	2000/6560	7	■				
La Pinilla	1500/4920	2273/7457	12	■	■			
El Port Ainé	1650/5413	2440/8005	6	■				
Port del Comte	1690/5544	2400/7874	15	■	■			
Puerto de Navacerrada	1700/5577	2222/7290	12	■				
San Isidro	1490/4888	2100/6890	12	■	■			
Sierra Nevada	2208/7244	3616/11863	19	■	■			
Super Espot	1490/4888	2320/7611	6	■				
Tuca-Mall Blanc	1000/3280	2250/7382	9	■	■			
Valcotos	1785/5856	2270/7477	8	■				
Valdesqui	1860/6102	2280/7480	11	■	■			
Valdezcaray	1550/5085	2263/7424	11	■	■			
Valgrande Pajares	1480/4855	1834/6017	13	■	■			

Key: beg = beginner, int = intermediate skier, adv = advanced skier, non = non-skier.
*Figures in brackets indicate approximate total number of lifts in adjoining valleys or within the same area for which a combined ski pass can be purchased.

| | Altitude (m/ft) | | No. | Recommended for: | | | | |
	Resort	Highest lift	of lifts*	beg	int	adv	non	Linked areas
SWEDEN								
Riksgränsen	472/1550	910/2985	6	(touring, heli-skiing)				
Åre	396/1300	1274/4180	40(48)	■	■	■		Duved
SWITZERLAND								
Adelboden	1400/4593	2350/7710	28(49)	■	■			Lenk
Andermatt	1447/4747	2961/9714	13			■		
Anzère	1430/4691	2460/8071	11		■			
Arosa	1800/5905	2655/8710	17	■	■		■	
Arolla	2000/6560	2889/9478	5	■	■			
Bettmeralp	1950/6397	2709/8888	14	■	■			
Celerina	1730/5676	3057/10029	25	■	■			
Champéry	1040/3412	2320/7611	20(162)	■	■			Portes du Soleil
Champoussin	1680/5512	2350/7710	25(162)	■	■			Portes du Soleil
Château d'Oex	1000/3280	1750/5741	16	■	■			
Crans Montana	1500/4920	3000/9842	42	■	■		■	
Davos	1560/5118	2844/9331	47(73)	■	■	■	■	Klosters
Les Diablerets	1151/3776	3000/9842	19(60)		■			Villars/Leysin
Engelberg	1040/3412	3020/9908	25	■				
Falera	1218/3996	3018/9901	32	■	■			
Flims/Laax	1150/3773	3018/9901	34	■	■			
Grindelwald	1120/3674	2970/9744	15(44)	■	■			Jungfrau
Gstaad	1051/3448	3000/9842	15	■	■			
Haute Nendaz	1365/4478	3330/10925	21(100)	■	■	■		Quatre Vallées
Klosters	1130/3707	2844/9330	26(73)		■	■		Davos
Lenk	1070/3510	2330/7644	21(49)	■	■			Abelboden
Lenzerheide	1465/4806	2865/9399	13(39)	■	■			Valbella
Leukerbad	1411/4629	2700/8858	17	■	■			
Leysin	1200/3937	2300/7546	13(60)	■	■			Villars/Les Diablerets
Morgins	1375/4511	2102/6896	23(162)	■	■			Portes du Soleil
Mürren	1650/5413	2970/9744	14(44)	■	■			Jungfrau
Pontresina	1920/6299	3616/11863	12	■	■			
Saas Fee	1800/5905	3600/11811	26	■	■	■	■	
Saas Grund	1560/5118	3100/10170	21	■	■			
St Moritz	1830/6004	3300/10827	59		■	■	■	
Verbier	1500/4920	3330/10925	44(100)		■	■		Quatre Vallées
Villars	1253/4111	2970/9744	28(60)	■	■		■	Les Diablerets/Leysin
Wengen	1280/4199	2486/8157	15(44)	■	■			Jungfrau
Zermatt	1620/5315	3895/12778	36(73)	■	■	■		Cervinia
Zinal	1670/5479	2900/9514	9	■	■			
TURKEY								
Uludag	2543/8343	2583/8474	13	■				

Key: beg = beginner, int = intermediate skier, adv = advanced skier, non = non-skier.
*Figures in brackets indicate approximate total number of lifts in adjoining valleys or within the same area for which a combined ski pass can be purchased.

| | Altitude (m/ft) | | No. | Recommended for: | | | | |
	Resort	Highest lift	of lifts*	beg	int	adv	non	Linked areas
UNITED STATES								
Alta, UT	2605/8546	3216/10551	9		■	■		
Arapahoe, CO	3287/10784	3978/13050	5(55)		■	■	■	Summit County
Aspen, CO	2438/7998	3596/11800	42(58)		■	■	■	Snowmass
Beaver Creek, CO	2471/8107	3489/11447	10(34)	■	■			Vail
Breckenridge, CO	2926/9600	3964/13005	16(55)	■	■	■	■	Summit County
Cannon Mountain, NH	577/1893	1277/4189	6		■	■		
Copper Mountain, CO	2926/9600	3767/12359	20(55)	■	■			Summit County
Crested Butte, CO	2857/9375	3707/12162	13		■	■		
Crystal Mountain, WA	1340/4396	2134/7001	10		■	■		
Grand Targhee, WY	2420/7939	3160/10367	4		■			
Heavenly Valley, CA/NE	2194/7200	3080/10102	25	■	■			
Jackson Hole, WY	1924/6312	3187/10456	10		■	■		
Keystone, CO	2836/9304	3651/11978	23(55)	■	■			Summit County
Killington, VT	672/2205	1294/4245	19	■	■	■		
Kirkwood, CA	2385/7825	2996/9829	10			■		
Lake Placid, NY	294/964	1356/4449	9		■	■		
Loon, NH	274/899	915/3002	9		■			
Mammoth Mt, CA	2745/9000	3371/11060	30	■	■			
Mount Snow, VT	504/1653	1087/3566	18	■	■			
Park City, UT	2104/6903	3052/10013	13	■	■	■		
Snowbird, UT	2470/8100	3354/11000	8	■	■	■		
Snowmass, CO	2505/8218	3590/11778	16(58)	■	■			Aspen
Solitude, UT	2666/8747	3343/10968	7		■	■		
Squaw Valley, CA (Lake Tahoe)	1896/6220	2758/9048	38		■	■		
Steamboat, CO	2105/6906	3203/10508	21	■	■	■		
Stowe, VT	504/1653	1344/4409	10	■	■		■	
Sugarbush, VT	496/1627	1227/4025	12	■	■			
Sugarloaf, MA	487/1598	1290/4232	13	■	■	■		
Sun Valley, ID	1752/5748	2790/9153	16		■			
Sundance, UT	1860/6102	2500/8202	4		■	■		
Taos, NM	2806/9206	3602/11817	10			■		
Telluride, CO	2792/9160	3805/12483	10	■	■			
Vail, CO	2500/8202	3491/11453	24(34)	■	■	■	■	Beaver Creek
Waterville Valley, NH	474/1555	1183/3881	11	■	■			
Winter Park, CO	2746/9010	3676/12060	20	■		■		

Thanks to Patrick Thorne of Snowhunter, and to Asako Sato and Yoichi Sasakawa.

Annual reference books such as *The Good Skiing Guide* or the *Volvo Ski Guide* provide further information.

USEFUL SOURCES OF INFORMATION

GREAT BRITAIN

General information, kindred spirits
SKI CLUB OF GREAT BRITAIN
118 Eaton Square
London SW1W 9AF
071 245 1033

Involvement and competition
ENGLISH SKI COUNCIL
Area Library Building
Queensway Mall
The Cornbow, Halesowen
West Midlands B63 4AJ
021 501 2314

SCOTTISH NATIONAL SKI COUNCIL
Caledonia House
South Gyle
Edinburgh EH12 9DQ
031 317 7280

SKI COUNCIL OF WALES
240 Whitchurch Road
Cathayes
Cardiff CF4 3ND
0222 619637

BRITISH SKI FEDERATION
258 Main Street
East Calder
West Lothian EH53 OEE
0506 884343

Other useful organisations
BRITISH ASSOCIATION OF SKI INSTRUCTORS
Inverdruie Visitors Centre
Grampian Road, Aviemore
Inverness-shire PH22 1RL
0479 810 407

BRITISH SNOWBOARD ASSOCIATION
55 Priory Avenue
Taunton
Somerset TA1 1X2
0823 272461

Skiing for people with disabilities
BACK-UP
The Business Village
Broomhill Road
London SW18 4JQ
081 871 5180/1

BRITISH SKI CLUB FOR THE DISABLED
Springmount
Berwick St John
Shaftesbury
Dorset SP7 0HQ
0747 828 515

THE UPHILL SKI CLUB
12 Park Crescent
London W1N 4EQ
071 636 1989

CANADA

CANADIAN SKI ASSOCIATION
1600 James Naismith Drive
Gloucester, Ontario K1B 5N4
613 748 5660

CANADIAN SKI INSTRUCTORS' ALLIANCE
774 Boul Decarie, Suite 310
St Laurent, Quebec H4L 3L5
514 748 2648

CANADIAN ASSOC. FOR DISABLED SKIING
PO Box 307
Kimberley
British Columbia V1A 2Y9
604 427 7712

UNITED STATES OF AMERICA

PROFESSIONAL SKI INSTRUCTORS OF AMERICA
133 South Van Gordon Street
Suite 240
Lakewood, Colorado 80228
303 987 9390

SKI INDUSTRIES ASSOCIATION OF AMERICA
8377-B Greensboro Drive
McLean, Virginia 22102
703 556 9020

UNITED STATES SKI ASSOCIATION
1500 Kearns Blvd-HWY 248
PO Box 100
Park City, Utah 84060
801 649 9090

NATIONAL HANDICAPPED SPORTS ASSOC.
4405 East West Highway
Suite 603
Bethesda, Maryland 20814
301 652 7505

OTHER COUNTRIES

INTERNATIONAL SKI FEDERATION (FIS)
Blochstrasse 2
CH-3653 Oberhofen/Thunersee
Switzerland
33 44 61 61

OESTERREICHISCHER SKIVERBAND
Olympiastrasse 10
Innsbruck A-6020
Austria
512 59 50 10

FÉDÉRATION FRANÇAISE DE SKI
50 rue des Marquisats
BP 451, 74011 Annecy Cedex
France
50 51 40 34

SCHWEIZERISCHER SKI-VERBAND
Worbstrasse 52
CH-3074 Muri b. Berne
Switzerland
31 52 52 11

Index